When Trying to Change Him Is Hurting You

DR. DAVID HAWKINS

HARVEST HOUSE PUBLISHERS

EUGENE, OREGON

Cover by Koechel Peterson & Associates, Inc., Minneapolis, Minnesota

This book includes stories in which the author has changed people's names and some details of their situations to protect their privacy.

WHEN TRYING TO CHANGE HIM IS HURTING YOU

Formerly titled *Men Just Don't Get It—But They Can*
Copyright © 2003 by David Hawkins
Published by Harvest House Publishers
Eugene, Oregon 97402
www.harvesthousepublishers.com

Library of Congress Cataloging-in-Publication Data
  Hawkins, David, 1951-
    [Men just don't get it—but they can]
    When trying to change him is hurting you / David Hawkins.
        p. cm.
    Includes bibliographical references.
    ISBN-13: 978-0-7369-1698-1 (pbk.)
    ISBN-10: 0-7369-1698-9 (pbk.)
  1. Marriage—Religious aspects—Christianity. 2. Man-woman relationships—Religious aspects—
  Christianity. I. Title.
  BV835.H378 2006
  248.8'435—dc22   2005028090

Printed in the United States of America

06 07 08 09 10 11 12 13 / BP-CF / 10 9 8 7 6 5 4 3 2 1

*This book is dedicated to the many women
who have entrusted me with their painful stories,
with the hope and belief that the secrets in this book
will help them live fuller and richer lives.*

Acknowledgments

Creating a book takes a tremendous amount of work and is accomplished with the help of a lot of people. I want to acknowledge a few of them here.

My book begins with a dream—a dream that comes from seeing a need that can be met through writing. I want to first thank Terry Glaspey, Director of Acquisitions at Harvest House Publishers, for catching the vision of this book. He not only believed in this book and assisted me in crafting its direction but also has shown repeatedly that he believes in me. Thank you, Terry.

Terry introduced me to Gene Skinner, who has faithfully worked with me through a number of revisions. Gene is very gifted at gently offering helpful suggestions while standing back and allowing me to determine the ultimate direction of the book. Thankfully, I am working with him on another project, and I am delighted that he is on my team.

I also want to thank the entire staff at Harvest House Publishers. They have shown me in countless ways that they are a quality publishing firm, one I am so proud and grateful to be a part of. Let's keep this thing going.

Special thanks go to Jim and Christie, who tirelessly read through chapter after chapter, asking me probing questions, offering suggestions, and always encouraging me. I appreciate your support.

Finally, I want to thank my parents, Hank and Rose, who have always encouraged me to write. They have always believed in me and known that I had a passion that needed to be heard. Thanks, Mom and Dad.

Contents

A Note from the Author

Many men and women have granted me a privileged position in their lives. They invite me behind closed doors, into their anger, pain, confusion, and, too rarely, happiness. As a clinical psychologist, I do not take this invitation lightly. These people are often desperate, aching for a comforting word. They listen intently to what I have to say. I give advice sparingly and with due consideration.

In the past several years, I have noticed troubling patterns of behavior that seem to amplify women's relational difficulties. Fortunately, thoughtful responses to these patterns can end long-standing destructive styles of relating. These new responses (or *secrets*) can free women to behave in different ways and open the door to new, life-giving results.

I have seen women scream out in frustration. They withdraw into silence. They cry and wonder if they will ever feel appreciated and respected. They use a tremendous amount of energy wishing their partner would change. Sadly, most of their energy is wasted because they do not utilize it for positive change. This book will clearly show how women unwittingly enable men to avoid making the very changes they are seeking.

When Trying to Change Him Is Hurting You will help those who have all but given up on a mutually beneficial relationship. It will clearly describe useful tools that women can use to make radical changes in their marriage. Instead of feeling stuck in a relationship where they are ignored, devalued, unappreciated, and perhaps abused, they will find the spark that can ignite significant change in their partners. At the very least, they will find better lives for themselves.

One might ask why women should have to be the ones to motivate their partners to change. Aren't men supposed to be the godly leaders in the home? Unfortunately, men often do not stand up and provide responsible, loving leadership. But then, they are often let off the hook by their spouses in this area of family leadership. Of course men are responsible to grow up and "get it" in their relationships. However, we all know that most people do not change without an impetus to do so. Women can often provide that impetus. They are not responsible to make men change, but they can powerfully influence men to alter their immature behaviors. That is precisely what I hope they do after reading this book.

And what is God's role in this process? Are you to do this all on your own using sheer willpower? Of course not. Our God is not some far-off deity who is beyond the reach of our daily needs. We do not fling up a prayer and hope that it eventually makes its way to the top of His "To Do" list. However, He is also not a genie in a bottle that we rub to instantly get what we want in life. God has promised to be available to offer wisdom, compassion, and guidelines for how we are to conduct ourselves in difficult situations.

God has given us the ability to think, and women will need to think through the changes suggested in this book. He has also given us courage to make difficult choices. Listen to God's voice and receive strength from Him as you embark on this journey. Be prepared for a new and exciting life. If you follow the advice provided in this book, that is what you will get.

One

The Lies We Believe

*Our recognition and apprehension
of the highest truth is essentially an affair
of the heart, far more than of the head.*

J.S. KIEFFER

"The truth will set you free."

Perhaps you have never given that scriptural maxim a lot of thought, but it is the foundation of this book. And though the truth can set us free, it can also be dangerously evasive. We can easily lose our way and believe subtle distortions of the truth that eventually create havoc in our lives.

For most of us, the truth is never more relevant than when it pertains to creating healthy, happy relationships. When our relationships are not doing well, we are not doing well. By actively seeking truth, you can positively impact those relationships and make them much more fulfilling.

You probably picked up this book because the title caught your eye. Somebody in your life doesn't seem to "get it." The relationship may appear very normal and possibly quite gratifying in many ways. But something is missing. Perhaps a vitality in your marriage is missing that you would like to rediscover. Perhaps the honesty, trust, or passion has faded. This book can help you understand what is missing and develop ways to recreate that healthy relationship you desire.

This book promises to reveal "secrets every woman should know." These secrets will empower you—not to manipulate your partner into changing, but to alter the way you view your problems and choose to behave. Each secret will enable you to build a larger world where change becomes ever more possible. And each secret is built upon this fundamental premise: You must tell yourself the truth, and that truth will help you to make better, healthier decisions. Indeed, the truth can make you free.

This book is primarily for women whose marriage or primary relationship is not working as they dreamed it would. Feelings of disappointment are too familiar. You aren't ready for divorce court; you simply want more. Thankfully, you can have more. You have already made attempts to change your love relationship but to no avail. You have encouraged your partner to grow—even nagged at him—but have run into excuses, resistance, stubbornness, or perhaps even outright belligerence. In these pages you will find another opportunity to evaluate what is wrong and to determine what *you* can do to improve things.

This book is about finding answers, not assigning blame. Pointing fingers at the man in your life would be easy. Why isn't he being the leader of your home, as is his rightful duty? Why does he proclaim the truth on Sundays, only to recant on Monday morning? At times you feel like telling people that he is not what they perceive him to be. Of all his shortcomings, the worst may be his resistance to change.

This book, however, is not ultimately about his refusal to change. If you bog down in the things that he does wrong, you will remain hopelessly stuck in the same old place. Yes, we will talk about him, but ultimately *this book is about you*. It is about the lies that you have believed that keep you doing the same things you have done in the past and getting the same insufficient results. This book is about finding real answers for creating change in your love relationship. It is about enjoying all that God wants for your marriage. And He wants a great deal for you.

Together we will focus on the lies that you believe that are keeping your life stagnant. These are the lies you have accepted and lived by much of your life. The ones that say your relationship is good enough, that things are not that bad, that you can change him, or that you will never have an extraordinary relationship. Most importantly, this book is about confronting those lies and being truthful with yourself. "And the truth will set you free." In this book you can discover new truths, nine secrets that will revolutionize your interactions with the man in your life in new and powerful ways. God has a wonderful life in store for you. He does not want you to live in a relationship that is mediocre at best.

You can find lasting, loving change in your relationship. But the way is littered with obstacles; in many cases, these are the various ways you enable your partner to not change. That is precisely why the focus will be on you, not on him. I will dare you to look deeper, past the easy explanations. I will confront you, challenge you, and perhaps even annoy you. I will encourage you to consider alternative approaches to your relationship and try them on for size.

So, understanding that you will need to look at how you have been misusing your energies, and knowing that change can only occur after you have faced the truth and made a plan to deal with it, let's begin.

> "For I know the plans I have for you," declares the
> LORD, "plans to prosper you and not to harm you,
> plans to give you hope and a future" (Jeremiah 29:11).

Randy and Carla

Carla was a 27-year-old woman who came to my office after months of anxious deliberation. She was generally happy but had noticed that she no longer bounced out of bed with her usual vigor. She had a reputation for being the life of the party, one who could easily make others laugh. Her smile was quick, her sense of humor contagious.

Her colleagues at the advertising agency where she worked sensed something was troubling her. "Where is the chipper old Carla?" they asked. She hadn't realized the change was that obvious.

Her husband, Randy, sensed it too. Their level of intimacy had dropped, and he felt rejected. Carla didn't seem interested in sex anymore, and when they were intimate, she seemed to approach lovemaking as an obligation. When Randy became angry, he pushed her away, creating even more distance between them. She had tried to tell him that she was dissatisfied with their relationship, that she was tired of being treated like a housekeeper and childcare provider instead of a full partner in their relationship. But she felt as if Randy simply didn't listen. Her resentment grew.

"I don't know why I'm here," she began. "I just about cancelled, but I figured I might as well come and see if this can help me in some way."

"So, what would you like help with?" I asked.

"I'm really not sure. I just know that I'm not as happy as I used to be. But I can't seem to put my finger on anything that would cause me to be unhappy."

"Maybe we should do a little exploring to see if we can find the culprit."

"I don't even know where to begin."

People often tell me that they do not know what is bothering them when in fact they have a very good idea. We seem to want to push issues to the backs of our minds. Maybe we believe that if they are out of sight, they will be out of mind. By listening closely to ourselves—which takes a great deal of practice and patience—we can discover what we need to change.

"Do you have any idea what might be troubling you?" I asked.

"Well, I'm often angry at my husband, but I'm not sure why. I keep asking for help around the house and help with the kids, and all I get are a bunch of excuses. I work 40 hours a week, I do the grocery shopping, I take care of the house, and I deal with the kids' problems. He tells me he's busy too, working full-time and trying to keep our finances in order. He has a thousand reasons why he can't help, and I resent it. I'm tired and I need a hand. This has been going on for years, and I need things to change."

"So what do you do about it? It sounds like a simple problem but one that could grow larger if you don't address it."

"I tell him that I need help, he gets defensive and makes excuses, and we drop the subject. Randy is a really good man. He's kind and caring in other ways. I don't want to make it sound like he is lazy or mean—he's not. But when it comes to helping me manage the daily activities of the home, he seems preoccupied with his stuff. I don't know what else I can do."

Carla swiveled in her chair and looked out the window. She bit her lower lip and closed her eyes for a moment. I expected her to start crying, but she didn't. Or wouldn't.

"It can be very frustrating," I said, "when you want changes but realize that making them takes so much energy. I bet you ask yourself if it's worth all the bickering."

"I start to fight with him and then give up. One thing I've learned from our marriage is that arguing is not going to change anything. But why does working out these problems have to be such a big deal? I've been working full-time, taking care of the kids, cooking, and cleaning the house for years. I'm exhausted! I threaten to quit work to take care of the kids and house, and he tells me I'd be neglecting my responsibilities as a wife if I did that. It makes me so mad. All I want is a little help."

Healthy People, Unhealthy Marriage

Can two relatively healthy people share a relatively unhealthy marriage? The answer is yes. Partners can function quite effectively in different aspects of their lives, such as work and friendships, and yet fail to develop an enriching relationship in their marriage. How is this possible?

Marriage and relational commitment require something different from friendship. That statement may seem like a no-brainer, but it is worthy of consideration. In committed relationships we let our hair down, fail to put away our dirty towels, and leave unpleasant stuff in the sink for our partner to clean up. Sadly, we often fail to bring our best selves to the table, and this inevitably takes its toll.

In marriage we must dig a little deeper into ourselves to meet the needs of our partner. Friendship and work relationships require only occasional efforts at being emotionally available. Marriage takes day-in and day-out relational commitment. We must be emotionally engaged on an ongoing basis in order for intimacy to thrive.

Marriage experts Drs. Les and Leslie Parrott speak to this issue in their book *Saving Your Marriage Before It Starts*. They report that couples are more often intimate with close friends than they are with their partners. Women often seek out friends before they confide in their husbands. They stress the importance of being best friends with one another, adding "not really listening is the fundamental error couples make."[1] The impact that these patterns have on committed relationships can be disastrous.

We must work to maintain intimacy, or resentments will grow and the relationship will dissolve. The ties that keep the marriage together often slowly unravel, leaving fragmented pieces. We must pay daily attention to the ongoing and ever-changing demands of the relationship.

Marriage requires an increased ability to manage conflict in a healthy way. Because you and your partner share the same sinks and toilet paper dispensers, not to mention the same cars and money, you will have more opportunities for conflict and challenges. Friendship often does not face these same tests of patience.

The Safety of Deception

We hope that change will occur, that our lives will evolve and take on new meaning, but we are also scared to death that change will sweep away the comfortable pieces of our lives that we have painstakingly assembled. Most of us spend years building our personal fortresses of daily routines, coping strategies, and safe friendships. Each day we conveniently hop over the moat of conflicts we've ignored, relationships we've starved, and dreams we've drowned. One day, the enemy—often in the form of dissatisfaction or depression—hauls a siege tower up to our fortress walls and starts firing boulders into our lives. Until then, nothing is quite as safe as the world we have constructed.

We may attempt to ignore the onslaught, but a time comes when we can no longer dance around the boulders. Action becomes frighteningly necessary.

Carla desperately wants to change her world and yet has grown quite accustomed to it. She has grown used to her home, her children's hugs after work, eating dinner as a family. She fears the repercussions of a more intense confrontation. She wonders if she really is as unhappy as she believes. Perhaps she is exaggerating her feelings. Perhaps her husband is really the more reasonable of the two. After all, how can she be sure that she is not manufacturing some of her trouble? Perhaps he is right about "wifely duties."

As I listened to Carla, I encouraged her to voice the many sides of the struggle. I learned long ago that our lives are intricate tapestries not easily understood or unwoven. Carla had no pat answers for her future. She knew, in spite of her wishes to the contrary, that the complexities of her life could not be simplified in a therapeutic hour. She needed time to voice her fears and frustrations. Having done so, she would then be prepared to make some decisions that were best for her.

One of my first tasks was to help her see that she could make many adjustments and to convince her that Randy might change if she, and then they, could understand their ruinous patterns. She would have to recognize how attached she was to her old way of relating to him. She would have to let go of any tendencies to see either herself or him as the entire problem. Both played a role in this hurtful and destructive pattern of relating.

Perhaps you see yourself in Carla and Randy's life. You are familiar with the many voices, the many parts of yourself. You know quite well how complicated you are. You also know, intuitively, that it is not all about him. You know in your heart that you must make changes to the only person you can fully control: yourself. And then you must hold him up in prayer and trust that the changes you make, with the work of the Holy Spirit, will bring about the transformation you seek. This process will not be without pain or risks.

Carla was generally happy in her marriage and thankful for the strengths they had, but she did have moments of intense frustration. She could not help but wonder what would happen if Randy refused to change. These kinds of thoughts are perfectly normal in any marriage, but our focus must be on improving and healing marriages, not severing them.

Thomas Moore, in his insightful book *Care of the Soul,* talks about the daunting fear of ending a relationship that has lost its vibrancy. "The thought of separating enters the minds of many people living a pact of love. But the thought is not the same as literal action. The idea of separation might suggest many things about the love, but the act means only one thing: the destruction of the relationship in its current form."[2]

Perhaps this feeling of destruction, and the fear of unleashing the floodwaters of consequences, was what brought Carla back to the reality that her marriage really was worth saving and that she and Randy could solve their problems. All she had known, all she had created, could be destroyed in one fell swoop if she were to follow through with her fleeting desire to get away from Randy. She reminded herself to keep their problems in perspective. She had to find a way to get through to him. What were some new ways of reaching him? How could she truly let him know that things had to change?

Painful Discussion

Several weeks later, after they'd finished dinner, Carla worked up the courage to confront her husband. "Randy, we need to talk. I'm tired of being mistreated. I have tried to talk to you, but it just doesn't work. I don't know if it's you or me, but whatever it is we're doing, it's not working. I think we need professional help. I want both of us to go to counseling to see if there is some way we can change things."

Randy pushed away from the table, obviously annoyed. He had this conversation with Carla before, and he was in no mood to revisit it.

"I don't see why you have to keep harping about this counseling thing. It isn't necessary. Our marriage is just like every other. You want what you see in the movies, and you can't handle the fact that real marriages don't work that way. You need to realize that this is our life, and it's not as bad as you think. I'm not exactly thrilled with the way you treat me either. I don't like being reminded of how I'm failing as a husband. Did you ever consider that you play a pretty big role in our problems too? And you can forget about the shrink. I don't think we need a stranger telling us how to live our lives."

Randy got up and walked into the living room, grabbed the newspaper, and plopped down on the couch. Carla began to cry but kept her sobs quiet, so she wouldn't upset Randy any more or worry the children, who were watching television in the basement. She wondered if they had heard her and Randy fighting. She and Randy had always conducted their battles quietly, but she wondered more frequently if the children knew their parents were not getting along. The harder she held on to her tears, the more they seemed to burst from her. She knew very well that Randy hated for her to cry and would become even angrier if he saw her. She fought to control her tears as she busied herself with cleaning the kitchen.

Conversations like this take place in millions of homes every evening with the same ending. Sometimes the woman withdraws into silence, sometimes the man. As you can see, Carla and Randy did not resolve the problem. In fact, they ignored it, and Randy used a litany of distractions to keep Carla from getting to the heart of the problem. And despite my conversations with Carla, she fell back into her old ways of relating to Randy. Let's dissect the conversation to see how destructive it was and examine the tactics used to make any real resolution impossible.

Randy became angry. This can deter many women from pursuing an issue. Most learn to fear anger, or worse, to anticipate that even more anger may be coming. Many women fear tension of any kind in their home. Taught to be people pleasers, they often want peace in their home at any expense. In this case, the cost is high and the results are disastrous.

Randy diverted the blame onto her. She was the one that was "harping" on things. She would not let things be. She kept prodding a touchy issue, and Randy wanted no part of it. What better way to avoid the problem than to convince her that she is a nag?

Randy tried to get Carla to feel as if her expectations were unrealistic. According to Randy, Carla lives in dreamland because her ideas about marriage are nothing but a romantic illusion, far removed from the daily world of bills and braces. All marriages have these problems. Professional help is unnecessary.

Randy made Carla feel as if her solutions were ridiculous. Going to "a shrink" is a way for Randy to ridicule Carla and make her feel even more insecure about her expectations. She is already unsure of what needs to change, and Randy found an easy and vulnerable target to drive home his spite. Sure enough, Carla walked away feeling powerless, hopeless, and confused. His weapons had hit the bull's-eye.

That night, he emerged the victor, though of course in the end he may lose the love and respect of his partner—a tall price to pay for his insecurities.

Enabling

We dare not criticize Carla for avoiding a difficult encounter with Randy and trying to cope in the only ways she knows. But as we watch her busy herself in the kitchen we want to shout to her, "Keep fighting, Carla. Don't let him get away with treating you that way. Don't let him intimidate you and then saunter off to the comforts of the couch and newspaper. Don't do it!"

But taking action is easier said than done. Carla has been enabling Randy for a long time. Carla has some sense that things in their marriage are causing severe problems, but caught in a swirl of confusion, she believes she has little ability to change them. She drifts back into old ways of ineffective relating. Employing the secrets in the following chapters as well as seeking the truth through prayer and godly counsel will provide the power that will drive change. Godly truth will guide you toward necessary change, but enabling will hinder you from making progress. And enabling is a central focus of this book, the major problem our secrets are designed to change.

So, what is enabling? Enabling is anything you do or do not do, say or do not say, that allows things to stay the same. When Carla walked away from Randy, allowing him to gloat in the living room, she was enabling him to behave just the way he had behaved for years. When she tolerated his angry outburst, she sent him the message that he could be angry and say whatever he wanted to say. When she slipped into confusion, she let him know, indirectly, that his words were powerful enough to befuddle her. As Carla grows she will learn to be firm in speaking the truth. She will not walk away but will stand firm in that truth and hold out for reasonable negotiation.

Randy uses anger because it works for him. He is not about to give it up as long as he can employ it to get what he wants. It is enough, at this stage of our work, to begin to see his tactics and plan strategies for dealing with them. These strategies involve changing *you*, with the understanding that changing *you* provides your best chance of changing *him!*

Remember, you are only responsible for changing you, not him. And if you change you, the worst that can happen is that you will become a happier and healthier person. God willing, your husband may change in the process. If he doesn't, then perhaps you will need to take more decisive steps.

Consider all the ways you have enabled (allowed things to stay exactly the same). Think of all the times you have...

- walked away because you were afraid of making him angry
- busied yourself so as to not think about how unhappy you are
- justified your unhappiness by telling yourself that things are not that bad and could be a lot worse
- told yourself that if you are patient, he will change
- told yourself that you expect too much of him
- told yourself that you are suffering for your spiritual faith
- told yourself, *I am the problem*

Each of these behaviors is an example of you enabling your relationship to stay exactly the same. Each is carefully designed to not rock the boat. But do you really want to live on that boat any longer?

Being True to Yourself

Unfortunately, being true to yourself and understanding your unique and special needs is not a prescription for changing your partner. Being honest about who you are, knowing what is important to you, understanding God's will, and living by His values will surely bring you greater peace of mind. However, in no way do these things ensure that your partner will wake up and embrace change. Positive change is likely to occur in your relationship if you follow the course I prescribe, but you should double-check your motives before embarking on a path of personal growth. Your highest priority should be to live according to your own core values.

Dr. Harriet Goldhor Lerner, in her wonderful book *The Dance of Intimacy,* says we must repeatedly remind ourselves that trying to change our partners is fruitless. It leads to no change whatsoever in the relationship. Rather, what is required is a...

> ...transformation of consciousness, a different worldview than from what comes naturally. I refer here to the challenge of truly appreciating how little we can know about human behavior and how impossible it is to be an expert on the other person....We cannot know how and when another person is ready to work on something and how she or he will tolerate the consequences of change....As we become less of an expert on the other, we become more of an expert on the self. As we work toward greater self-focus, we become better able to give feedback, to share our perspective, to state clearly our values and beliefs and then stand firmly behind them.[3]

This counsel is consistent with the profound teaching in Matthew 7. Here we read that we are not to look at the faults of others but rather to inspect our own motives and actions. "First take the plank out of your own eye, and then you will see clearly to remove the speck in your brother's eye" (Matthew 7:5). This does not mean that we are to have no opinion about the behavior of others. Quite the contrary. We are free to be truthful with ourselves and with our mates. However, we must first inspect our own behavior.

A recent book by Don Miguel Ruiz called *The Four Agreements* struck a chord with many people. Born into a family of healers in Mexico, Ruiz went to medical school and became a surgeon before a near-death experience caused him to write about the "agreements" that changed his life. While I do not accept all that he offers, I particularly like the first agreement in the book. Ruiz tells us that we must not go against ourselves, our deepest truths, or our best intentions. He says:

> Everything you feel or believe or say that goes against yourself is a sin. You go against yourself when you judge or blame yourself for anything.... Being impeccable with your word is the correct use of energy; it means to use your energy in the direction of truth and love for yourself....But, making this agreement is difficult because we have learned to do precisely the opposite. We have learned to lie as a habit of our communication with others and more importantly with ourselves. We are not impeccable with our word.[4]

By imploring us to be impeccable with our word, Ruiz is saying that we must be utterly true to ourselves and to our deeply held Christian values. We must spend time considering, pondering, knowing what is important to us and living by that truth. And eventually, we must be willing to take risks, believing that if we are perfectly true to ourselves, the rest of our lives, including our relationships, will prosper naturally. When Carla obsesses on changing Randy, she loses track of the powerful insight that she is only responsible for and able to change herself.

Being Salt and Light

The Scriptures talk about the importance of being who you are—salt and light. Notice in Matthew 5:13 that Christ does not say, "You can be salt," but rather "You *are* the salt of the earth." The next verse states, "You are the light of the world." You are to let your saltiness and light impact all of humankind, especially right at home in your marriage. You are not to hide your true identity. The world and your marriage need your salt and light.

The philosopher Epictetus once said, "You are a principal work, a fragment of God Himself. You have in yourself a part of Him. Why then are you ignoring your high birth?"[5]

Both partners in the marital dance must be candid with their thoughts and beliefs and daring enough to challenge each other to a higher calling. Each one must be exactly who he or she is, not putting on pretenses or hiding behind stubbornness and anger as Randy did. Risk is involved, but the new "salty" taste will be well worth it.

What Makes Him Tick?

Randy storms out of the kitchen and hides himself in the newspaper. Why? Why won't he stand before Carla and address the problem directly, searching for a solution that can be beneficial to both of them? This would give both of them space to be individuals and yet live in wonderful harmony with each other. But that did not happen. Instead, more bricks were stacked on the wall between them, leaving each to suffer in isolation.

I suspect Randy felt a number of emotions.

He felt threatened. His wife was not happy with his performance around the house even though he saw himself as a diligent, hard-working man. She poked at his ego, and he used his well-rehearsed tactic of withdrawal to cope with threats.

He felt angry. He felt that his wife's requests were unreasonable. He really did not think the problem was that serious. Of course, this is denial on his part, for the problem remains, and tomorrow is not likely to be any different.

He felt confused. What was the big deal? In denial, he convinced himself that this was her problem. If he ignored her, maybe the problem would just go away. But in his heart, he wondered if he needed to be more assertive and face her with his concerns.

He felt uncertain and afraid. What if she persisted with her demands? Would he be forced to change? What would he be required to change? He was content with his routines and not particularly interested in new challenges, especially on the home front.

He felt sad and rejected. Sitting alone in the living room was not his idea of a fun evening. He wanted true contact and intimacy with his wife, and this was no way to get it. He knew that he would most likely be stubborn and wait for her to make the first overture to him. They were in for a cold, silent evening.

Every Step Counts

Many struggles drain couples' energy. Round-robin fights appear to be so simple but go on and on. Conversations that start out clear end up muddy. "What was it we were fighting about?" so many couples ask once the smoke has finally cleared.

Keeping focused in the midst of such turmoil is hard. Discussing issues in a productive way requires serious effort. Encounters sometimes degenerate into power struggles that culminate in hurt feelings and the loss of intimacy. How can we create real change?

As you begin this journey, the trail ahead may appear perilous. The path is unfamiliar. Trust that you will find the truth, and it will make you free. Trust that God will provide wisdom for the journey ahead. Solomon confirms that "if you look for it as for silver and search for it as for hidden treasure, then you will understand the fear of the LORD" (Proverbs 2:4). If you look and listen, you will find the right books, the right friends, and the right teachers to help you take one important step at a time.

Paths are never straight and easy. Life has many starts, stops, twists, and turns. Plan on them. As you begin to acknowledge the truth about your marriage and about how you and your partner relate to each other, you may fumble about with new behaviors. You may try to be assertive only to slip back into passivity. You may try to confront irresponsible behavior only to revert to snide comments and passive-aggressive tactics. You are not traversing a smooth and easy trail.

As you learn to listen more carefully to yourself and to God, as you let go of the lies that hinder you, the best path will emerge before you. One step at a time, one moment at a time.

Now, let's explore the nine powerful secrets that will forever change your relationships for the better.

Two

Be Truthful with Yourself

*Love is the most terrible, and also the
most generous of the passions; it is
the only one that includes in its dreams
the happiness of someone else.*

J.A. KARR

Cindy curled under the covers as she watched Tim prepare for bed. They had 20 years together, a marriage filled with good times and bad. Their lives were woven together as high school sweethearts. In the years that followed, they raised four wonderful daughters. She lay there trying to remember life before Tim and had a hard time doing so. They literally grew up together.

She watched as he readied himself for bed. He had his routine: flipping on the TV, laying out the next day's work clothes, brushing his teeth, running a comb once through his hair, and slipping into his side of the bed. She smiled when she thought about the way he preferred the left side of the bed even when they were sleeping at a hotel or the home of a friend.

She tried to think of good things, but her mind continued to replay scenes from another day of feeling devalued, discounted. She wanted to cuddle. He wanted to watch *Sports Center*. Earlier, she tried to tell him her ideas for remodeling the family room. He complained that she didn't understand how complicated such a job could be. As usual, he treated her opinions like they were the romantic notions of a naïve child.

Tim fell asleep within minutes of his head hitting the pillow. Cindy lay awake next to him, wondering how he could sleep while she struggled to understand their relationship. Sometimes she wished he would suffer the way she suffered. She was amazed that he did not see how unhappy she was. She felt a great deal of tenderness for Tim, but at times like this she wondered if she'd made a mistake in marrying him. She had a hard time sorting out her anger from her affection. Even now, as angry as she was, she would gladly take him into her arms if he were to awaken and reach out to her. But Tim didn't stir. He slept peacefully as if nothing in the world was wrong with their marriage and their lives.

That is exactly what he had told her a hundred times or more. Despite what she knew in her heart to be true, Cindy had not yet accepted the first secret we will discuss in this book: *Be utterly honest with yourself about the problems.* If your relationship feels that bad, it usually *is* that bad. Instead of confronting the problem head-on, Cindy found herself wondering if perhaps Tim was right.

She lay there as she did every night, staring at the white ceiling tiles, hoping for some answer to descend from above. Surely, she'd told herself, if she trusted God more, Tim would change, or at the very least, she would feel peace about their situation. But Tim was not changing, nor did he show the slightest inclination to do so. Neither did peace rest in her heart. She had tried turning their communication problems over to God, but could not quit mulling them over. Was this one of those times she had read about when God appeared to be silent? Still, she clung to her faith, for it was the one sure thing in her life right now.

Tim seemed to have a clear defense strategy: Make her believe that she created problems where none existed. Insist that she always made issues out to be bigger than they actually were. He liked to compare her behavior to that of her mother, who was forever making "mountains out of molehills." He seemed to enjoy reminding Cindy about the time three years ago when she had cried because her two-dollar timer quit working while preparing a meal. Perhaps he was right; perhaps she overreacted about everything from two-dollar timers to Tim's obsession with watching sports.

When Cindy came to me for counseling she was reluctant to share her story. She felt it was not worthy of professional help. She didn't tell Tim she had come for the appointment because she feared what he would say. She saved up some extra money and came to the appointment secretly. This in itself showed a certain level of fear that concerned me. I shared with her the secret in this chapter: Be utterly truthful with yourself about the problems. If you do so, you are less likely to ignore the problems, minimize them, or exaggerate them.

The River of Denial

The doctor came into the room where I lay and stood by the edge of my bed. I'd had trouble breathing for months and was hospitalized for more testing. As my doctor approached, he seemed frightened of getting too close even though I had no contagion. He was a caring man with a no-nonsense approach. I appreciated that because I could always count on him to tell me the truth without sugarcoating it.

He told me that I had adult onset asthma. It was very treatable, he said, but would require rigorous care. I required medications at least for several weeks and perhaps for my entire lifetime. The condition was incurable—I would need to learn to live with it. He explained how my body might react to an asthma attack, ways to prevent such attacks, and what to do if they came. He did not tiptoe around the bad news. He simply laid out the truth.

His approach was similar to that of a psychiatrist with whom I once studied. After an evaluation that I was privileged to observe, he minced no words in telling the family what they needed to change if they wanted to raise a healthy, functioning child. I wanted to soften his words, and I cringed when he looked directly into the parents' eyes and explained how their behavior was affecting their son. But he laid out the truth for them. People came to him from miles around because they knew his reputation for identifying problems, deciphering them, and laying out the solutions. His job was to lay out the truth for his clients. His clients' job was to decide what to do with that truth.

Denial may not be a river in Egypt, but it moves just as swiftly and often overflows its banks. It is pervasive in many relationships and grows like a virulent cancer. Before long, it can be just as deadly.

We often associate denial with addictive or violent behaviors when in reality we all practice it on a daily basis. In fact, some forms of denial are actually good and helpful. Who would want to constantly carry the weight of all of life's difficulties and disappointments? But denial can also be very destructive.

Desperate for a way to make their world tolerable, many women find denial, or minimization, a useful tool. Denial makes the lies easier to believe; it becomes a warm blanket to cuddle in to soften the pain. Denial makes the daily suffering easier to bear. Who is not tempted to look for comfort wherever it may be found when things are going badly?

Denial is not only used as a defense against major issues, such as verbal or emotional abuse. It can also numb the dull ache of more subtle maladies. What do we say to Denise, another of my clients, who lives with her husband of 13 years and tries to ignore his foul language? She knows that he works at a lumber mill where that kind of language is commonplace. She knows that he is not a bad person because of it. But she is also embarrassed when he swears and is especially mindful of the impact his profanity is having on their two young sons, both of whom have already begun adopting it.

Her husband, Mike, is a very hard worker. He has been a loyal husband and a fine employee. He arrives 20 minutes early for his shift so that the man he is relieving can get out of the mill a few minutes early to be with his family. He is always willing to work a double shift if someone needs time off for a family function or special event. Mike's generosity is known throughout the mill.

For Mike and his coworkers, the job is a tremendous source of pride and identity. Few others know the difficulty of working in a dirty, cold lumber mill in all kinds of weather and conditions. Few men are capable of doing the physical work the job demands. To alleviate the boredom, they tell off-color jokes. This is a challenging setting for a clean-cut Christian man. Mike says he is doing his best to watch his language. But is he really doing his best? He rationalizes his profanity by saying that everyone at the mill uses "colorful language." It is just something that Denise will have to accept, he explains.

What is she to do? They have two sons, a nice rambler in the suburbs, an SUV and a late-model sedan, a small savings account, a growing retirement plan, and dreams for the future. They attend church on Sundays. Mike even teaches Sunday school on occasion. When her denial is working, she finds herself believing that things are really not that bad.

Whitewashed Tombs

Being utterly truthful is not just a problem for us today. It was a significant problem for some of the most outwardly religious people in Jesus' day. You may recall Jesus' stunning indictment of the religious leaders of the community.

> Woe to you, teachers of the law and Pharisees, you hypocrites! You are like whitewashed tombs, which look beautiful on the outside but on the inside are full of dead men's bones and everything unclean. In the same way, on the outside you appear to people as righteous but on the inside you are full of hypocrisy and wickedness (Matthew 23:27-28).

These were fighting words. Jews believed that touching graves made one unclean, so the exteriors of the graves were thoroughly scrubbed as a warning to stay away. This squeaky-clean finish looked good on the outside but hid decomposing bodies on the inside. Jesus admonishes us to be truthful in our inner parts and not to present a clean façade that will impress others.

When you set out to confront the dishonesty in your marriage, you must first be truthful with yourself. Have you looked at your part in the problem? Have you acknowledged that you might not be confronting the problem in the most candid way possible? Have you been content to apply coats of whitewash to the tomb-like areas of your relationship?

From the Outside Looking In

As you listen to the stories of Cindy, Tim, Denise, and Mike, you may have mixed reactions. Perhaps their problems seem minor. But over a long period of time small problems can feel monumental. The challenge is to be utterly truthful with yourself when assessing your problems.

Things may look black and white from our vantage point, but the view from inside a relationship is not nearly as monochromatic. If life were as simple as we often believe it to be, decisions would be easy. Solutions would jump out at us, and we would know instantly which to choose. But dealing with problems in a relationship is rarely that simple. Lives become inextricably bound together like a finely woven rope with frayed ends.

You may have promised yourself you would never tolerate some of the things that are happening in your own relationship, but now you are clinging to the only life you know. You may feel disgusted with your weakness. Angry at your confusion. You look in the mirror and ask, *Why is it so hard to change?* But destructive habits are hard to break, so you settle once again into the comfortable routine of denial. Your problems aren't that bad, you tell yourself. But this is not the life God intended you to live. He would have you face the truth about your problems.

Minimization

Minimization is a cousin of denial. It keeps us safe, stuck, and stagnant. We use it each time we look at a serious problem and label it as "not so bad." We acknowledge that a problem exists but minimize its magnitude. We all use minimization at one time or another to justify behavior we know is wrong. Men often use it to justify their bad behavior toward women.

Tim uses minimization to justify his behavior. He deftly turns things around so that Cindy feels like she is making too much out of what he calls a small matter.

"Things are not that bad, Cindy," he said when she tried to confront him about coming home late from work. "You always make something out of nothing, and that's why you have trouble sleeping. It has nothing to do with me. Get a grip!"

"You promised that you would be home by seven so that we could spend some time together. You also said that we were going to have dinner together at least twice this week. The kids were so excited about it. But you haven't been home for dinner in weeks. We need to spend time together if we're going to be a real family."

"Do you think I want to come home to this? I get sick of the accusations. The way you talk, you'd think I was a convicted felon. I stay at the office working hard to support our family and the lifestyle you enjoy. I'm not out robbing banks. Can we put this thing in perspective, please?"

She looked away, avoiding his glare but feeling the sting of his words. Could he be right? His work was stressful and time-consuming. Unlike some of her friends' husbands, Tim was not out singing karaoke in cocktail lounges. He sang solos in the church choir.

He was not unethical, immoral, or lacking integrity. What he lacked was sensitivity to her needs and emotions. He was not a good listener and seemed caught up in his own world most of the time. But he spent time with their children most evenings, even if they just played a game of Blinx on the X-Box, and he seemed genuinely interested in what was happening to them.

"Look," Cindy said. "I don't want to pick a fight about this. All I want is time with you. Can we agree on a plan for spending more time together? Real families sit down to dinner together and talk about the day."

"I never said I was against that. I just don't want to be on a leash. I didn't marry you to have another mother."

"How can you say I want you on a leash? I don't complain when you play golf or go fishing."

"But you always make it seem like you're letting me do things. I feel like you're trying to control me, and I'm not going to put up with it."

"Can we agree on at least a couple of nights a week for dinner? The kids want to see you and wonder why you aren't here. I'm tired of making excuses for you."

"Why don't we just play it by ear? You make dinner, and if I can make it I will. If not, don't make it a big deal. I spend time with all of you on the weekends, don't I? If it makes you feel better, I'll take the kids to the park on Sunday. Now give it a rest, please."

Tim grabbed a magazine and plopped down on the couch. The discussion was over. He obviously had all he could take of this topic. She was the problem. But Cindy knew better. Tim had not been living up to his responsibilities as a husband and father for a long time, and no matter how hard she tried, she could not make that go away.

In His Image

Quite miraculously, God created us with the capacity to tell the truth. Unfortunately, we are equally capable of being deceptive, thanks to Satan's foibles. But in the likeness of God we are capable of being truth-bearers.

The Scriptures tell us that we must approach the Lord in spirit and in truth. "God is spirit, and his worshipers must worship in spirit and in truth" (John 4: 24). Jesus went on to say that He *is* "the way and the truth and the life" (John 14:6). As we relate to our heavenly Father in a truthful, honest way, that honesty should spill over into our relationships with others. Our relationship to the Lord empowers us to tell the truth.

I remember visiting the Sistine Chapel in Rome. Throngs of people lined up as far as the eye could see for a chance to enter this holy place and to see some of the greatest paintings on earth.

As I moved closer and closer, my excitement grew. The bumping and shoving, the security guards attempting to control the crowd, they all seemed to raise the level of anticipation. As we finally entered the long chamber, high upon the ceiling was Michelangelo's rendition of creation, the magnificent moment when God made man in His likeness. A thinking, decisive, governing man. Dr. Paul Brand and Philip Yancey, in their book *In His Image,* give a delightful account of how we have been made in the image of God. "What God had in mind for us…is to be the chief bearers of His likeness in the world. As Spirit, He remains invisible on this planet. He relies on us to give flesh to that spirit, to bear the image of God."[1]

Sadly, sin disrupted the wonderful flow of truth in the Garden, and we seem to keep reliving that terrible experience. Things go well for a time, and then Satan appears on the scene to introduce deception into the idyllic scene. The apostle John says, "He [Satan] was a murderer from the beginning, not holding to the truth, for there is no truth in him. When he lies, he speaks his native language, for he is a liar and the father of lies" (John 8:44). We have struggled with lies and deception since the Garden of Eden.

Making Comparisons

The next morning, Cindy left for school, where she worked as a teacher's assistant. She felt like she had a hangover, a common feeling after their heated discussions.

"Stay focused," she prayed quietly. "Don't forget to breathe. Lord, help me keep my wits about me and give me peace in this situation. Show me the truth, please."

At these moments she was glad to have the perspective of her friends. Though she was careful not to tell just anyone about her marital problems, she had several people she could talk to about her struggles. They empathized with her troubles. However, they also encouraged her to hang in there, address the problems in a clear and direct manner, and seek healthy solutions. Avoiding the problem or telling herself that she should not feel the way she was feeling would lead down a dead-end road.

Her friends were also careful not to malign Tim. While they did not condone his lack of sensitivity, they did not fuel the fire by putting him down. Nothing could be gained by painting Tim as a "bad person" and Cindy as "all good." Her friends were wise enough to know that every situation is complex.

The disciplines of physics and family therapy share a principle called *equilibrium*. Matter in a state of unrest and families in distress tend to be in a state of *disequilibria*. They seek homeostasis. Being in a state of dis-ease is painful and distressing, so we look for ways to find peace within ourselves. After many lengthy discussions with her husband, Cindy found herself looking for ways to cope. One of her tools was to make comparisons.

She asked friends questions to try to gain another perspective. She looked at their relationships and compared them to hers. She spoke with her friend Sue about some of her recent problems.

"Sue, do you ever feel like Jim refuses to take responsibility for things?"

"We all try to dodge our responsibilities. And Jim has certainly done his share of that. It's been a thorny issue in our marriage, for sure. But because we have labeled it a problem and talked about it again and again, things have gotten better. It's taken a lot of hard work. We didn't get where we are in one giant step. He had a way of turning things back on me and denying any responsibility in the matter, whether it was whose turn it was to help the kids with math homework or who was responsible for folding the laundry. It drove me crazy at times. Men can be like that. But don't give up. They can change."

Cindy remembered the advice she received at the gym from her friend Marilyn, who was not a Christian. Marilyn's words left her more than a little shaken.

"Men just don't get it, Cindy. They are self-centered, don't care about others, and look out for only themselves. Tim is not about to change, no matter what you do. You can get angry, or you can just learn to live with it. It doesn't make any difference. My advice to you is get used to it."

On her drive home, Cindy wondered about Marilyn's advice. Was her assessment accurate? Cindy left the gym feeling more confused than she had been before their conversation. If she truly only had two choices, to be angry or to accept his bad behavior, she knew which she would choose. She would accept his behaviors and try to rationalize them as something that all men did. But she knew in her heart that Marilyn's advice was wrong, and she believed Tim really could change.

Helpmates

Cindy thought long and hard about Marilyn's advice. Accept the bad with the good. He'll never change, so quit fighting it. But what was her role as a wife when she could see things that truly needed to change? Surely God did not expect her to be a dutiful wife who kept her mouth shut in the midst of wrong behavior. That was not consistent with what she believed. God created her to understand things, to apply wisdom to her life, and to be a helpmate even when help was difficult to receive. *What is my role now?* she wondered.

She pulled out her worn Bible, the one her grandmother had given to her for confirmation. It was filled with yellow highlights and margin notes from countless sermons. Cindy lit a candle and plopped down in her favorite chair. Pulling a shawl over her shoulders, she reread Ephesians 5:22-33 and examined Paul's description of the godly marriage:

- The wife is to defer to her husband in love.
- The husband is the head of the home.
- The husband is to love his wife sacrificially.
- The husband must love his wife as he loves himself.
- The wife must respect her husband.

She pulled out her journal of notes and prayers. "Lord," she wrote, "I am willing to have a devoted relationship to my husband, but Tim does not seem willing. What would You like me to do? What can I do? Help me, Lord, because things are not falling into place, and I am really hurting."

Comparisons Can Be Destructive

As Cindy compared her marriage to the passage in Ephesians, she wondered what she was doing wrong. She felt guilty and ashamed. Surely if she had done things right Tim would be a different man. He would be like the husband Paul described in Ephesians.

Comparisons can help us or hurt us. When we look at how well off we are compared to those living in Third World countries, we quickly see that we should be grateful for what we have. Conversely, when we look at friends who are living in verbally and physically abusive relationships and say, "Ours is not so bad," we deceive ourselves. Living without true intimacy and acceptance can be just as painful as physical abuse. Comparisons are destructive when they lull us into a false sense of well-being.

- They convince us that things are not so bad when in fact they are.
- They are deceptive because they make us believe that all relationships are disappointing.
- They can cause us to settle for hurtful behavior.
- They can cause us to lower our standards.
- They can cause us to deny our true feelings.
- They can cause us to believe lies.

Comparisons can be as deceptive as whitewashed tombs when we tell ourselves that things could be a lot worse and we have no right to complain.

Scott Peck, in his book *The Road Less Traveled*, reminds us that sometimes feeling bad is a necessary part of our lives. Feeling this way is no fun, but it is often a prerequisite for change. Change does not come easily when we would rather escape feeling bad than confront problems. Rationalization, justification, minimization, and making comparisons, all forms of denial and deception, help us feel normal. They bring us back into equilibrium, if only temporarily.

As a youth, I stole candy from our neighborhood grocery store. I was scared to death that I would be caught, and sure enough, I was. Being apprehended by the store owner was bad; facing my parents was even worse. I dreaded having to sit with my guilt and shame until I faced them. I wanted to get the whole thing over. In short, I didn't want to think about my plight or consider my responsibility for it.

When my parents heard about the ordeal, they were plenty angry. Their goal was to make sure that I felt bad. My goal was to hide, hurl, strike out, minimize—anything to get the focus off of me and get the ordeal over as soon as possible. I made outlandish comparisons to hardened criminals and said that all I had done was take something that would never be missed. Needless to say, this did not appease them.

My shoplifting experience illustrates the denial we all fall back on when facing pain. When bad things happen to us, we try to escape bad feelings any way we can. If we have not learned to "be with" these difficult emotions, the problem can intensify. Someone once said, "A feeling denied is intensified." Precisely.

We make comparisons to make ourselves feel better. However, this does not help us solve our problems and certainly does nothing to change our situation. Comparisons do not help us make the internal adjustments necessary for healthy relational change. Sadly, they only serve to help us cope temporarily with what is happening.

Coping

Coping is a way of keeping things tolerable. We can manage when we cope. But the bad news is that we don't become stronger. In many ways, coping is like a powerful sedative. It temporarily eases the pain but does little to provide real solutions.

Coping is making due with the status quo. If your relationship is troubled, you have probably learned how to find a reasonable equilibrium. Good for you! Managing your life in the face of adversity takes a lot of skill.

But I want to shake your world. I want to tell you that coping is not enough. In fact, coping is the enemy of deep personal growth, the antithesis of change. Coping—whether through denial, minimization, or other avoidant behaviors—lulls us into believing that all is okay. Like Cindy, we end up accepting that things are not that bad.

Shelly, a woman in her mid-forties, had clearly learned to cope—and she was miserable. Depressed, she was seeking a way out of her gloomy existence.

"I always thought that I was coping fairly well," Shelly said. "Doug still drinks every night, but he promises to cut back, and he does for a while. We'll fight and he'll complain, but he usually slows his drinking down. Then he picks back up again. Sometimes I wonder what my life would be like if I wasn't always fighting with him and if I had a partner who wanted intimacy like I do. But I cope. I give up my dreams of ever feeling a glow when we're together or seeing him as the white knight I can look to for understanding. Instead, I settle for the way things are. When I look at some of the things my friends are going through, my life with Doug does not seem that bad."

Things are not so bad, Shelly insists. "I'm coping." This is a line that we have heard others use, one that you may have used yourself. But beware. Danger lurks in those quiet places of temporary comfort.

Tunnel Vision

One of the problems with the big lie that "it's not that bad" is that comparisons are based on too little information. You ask the opinions of only a narrow group of friends, many of whom have never been in your shoes. Or you listen as the talk show gurus make generalizations about relationships and assert that trouble always results in adultery, abuse, and horrible anger.

You need useful, accurate information. The key is knowing where to get it. You must remind yourself of your true values, which should be based on scriptural truths and confirmed by the advice of stable and trustworthy friends. In fact, trusted friends...

- will not be overly opinionated
- will listen compassionately
- will help you process your current situation
- will understand and apply biblical truths
- will accept you no matter what you decide

You must reach out for support and valid information, but beware of constantly receiving information that is not useful. Instead of always asking advice of the same people, seek new perspectives. Best of all, listen to your heart and seek the wisdom of God.

My advice is to begin by thinking big. Perhaps your dreams are too small. Who said God can't give you the life you want? Who said your husband can't change? Who said you will melt into a puddle if you dare to make drastic changes? The time is now.

Comparisons Can Sometimes Heal

When we let fear control us, our options narrow. Fear constricts our vision and makes us hold on desperately to what we have even if what we are holding on to is less than satisfactory. We make comparisons that reinforce our worst fears when we say...

- Nobody has it any better than I do.
- Everybody is unhappy to some extent.

- Men can never change.
- I need to be happy with what I have.
- All men are the same.

These observations are narrow and irrational. They will not help you improve your relationship. Instead, they will leave you in a rut that is difficult to escape. However, other comparisons can heal. Jennifer's story illustrates this situation.

"I used to think that all men cheat, drink too much, and keep their feelings bottled up. That was my motto. I considered leaving my emotionally distant husband, but instead I went to counseling and began a deep search of myself. After I changed, I began to see the world differently. I decided that all men were not the same. I began looking harder for the exceptions rather than the so-called rule. I began to have 'possibility thinking.' I found some very satisfied women who have worked hard on their relationships and have created marriages filled with tenderness, kindness, and emotional availability. I decided to see what my husband and I could create together. It is possible!" And it started with being utterly truthful about the problems in their marriage.

What Makes Him Tick?

So, what makes Tim and Mike withdraw into silence? Why does Tim refuse to tune in to Cindy's reasonable request for more time and attention so that they can live in wonderful intimacy? The solution seems so simple, doesn't it?

For all of his wonderful qualities, Tim has never really learned the fine art of communication. Sharing his feelings is threatening for him. This is not unusual for men. They have not been schooled in sharing their inner hurts and desires. In fact, quite the opposite. Consider that men have been trained by their families and society to…

- be tough
- conquer

- solve problems
- hide their emotions
- talk about things and events, not feelings
- be practical, not relational and emotional
- guard their spiritual beliefs

Because of this, most men are at a distinct disadvantage in relationships. Since the beginning of civilization, men have been taught to be warriors, not whiners. And to many men, talking about relational problems feels a lot like whining. "Let's just get on with it. Do we have to talk and talk about this? Let's just get over it."

As a loving spouse, how can you help? Here are a few simple steps to try.

First, you can help by understanding that talking about relationships is challenging for men. This is a big stretch for them, so be understanding.

Second, you can teach men about feelings. Model the sharing of feelings for them. Don't go overboard, but in small doses show them how to share feelings.

Third, make men feel safe to share their feelings. Many men have had horrible experiences with sharing their hearts' desires. Be patient and listen to what they are trying to say, awkward as it might be.

Fourth, expect growth. Don't enable men to hide behind tradition and past experiences. They can and will grow, given the right circumstances.

Being Honest with Ourselves

If you are to arrive at your goal, you must be honest with yourself. For so long you have lived according to other people's truths. Your voice has gone silent—you barely know what you think. We must partner together to find your voice.

Patricia Evans, in her insightful book *Controlling People,* says:

> Having learned to deny their own wisdom and having taken in other people's definition of them, without even realizing it, those who are disconnected from themselves construct an identity not grounded in experience but constructed out of, or in reaction to, other people's ideas, expectations and values.[2]

You may have developed an identity built from the outside in, rather than from the inside out. When people tell you how to live, what to think, and what to feel, living from the inside out becomes nearly impossible. When you spend all of your energy trying not to make someone mad, or making sure your partner and children's needs are all met, finding the impetus to examine the quality of your own life seems like a luxury. Now is the time to stop living life according to other people's expectations. It's time to be an adult, one who controls her own destiny.

Growing new dreams first requires that you examine other choices than simply staying stuck. You must cross a bridge before you can arrive at a new destination. Open your eyes and look around. Take your eyes off him and what he has done, and recognize that you have lived a life of false beliefs. Other choices await you though you may not recognize them now. Moving forward does not have to mean leaving your relationship. To begin, moving forward can simply mean acknowledging the truth about yourself, your husband, and your relationship.

Please keep in mind that setting yourself free does not mean living outside the bounds of Christian mores. It means being far more responsible for your own behavior. When you spend time alone, thinking about what is important to you, prayerfully meditating on your values and dreams and then living accordingly, you live from the inside out. If our journey together teaches you anything, let it be this: You can only save one life, and that is your own.

The Wisdom of Denial

This book is about coming out of denial, shaking loose the lies that drag you down, but it is also about honoring the timing of your discovery of those truths. Many truths require time for gestation. They cannot be rushed and, ironically, often need the temporary cocoon of denial for them to grow from their embryonic fragility into hearty, wholesome expressions of wisdom that can stand on their own.

As you go through the painful process of re-membering, gathering into yourself those parts of you that you have tried to leave behind, be gentle. Be kind toward all that is unfinished in your heart. Honor the wisdom that has come from the place that you have traveled. One day you will know why life's events have occurred as they have. "We know only a portion of the truth, and what we say about God is always incomplete" (1 Corinthians 13:9 THE MESSAGE). One day as you look back you will say yes to all that has happened. You will recognize that all of your experiences have been a part of your necessary learning process, leading you to a fuller and richer life.

Three

Stop Making Excuses

You never find yourself until you face the truth.

Pearl Bailey

A group of frogs were thrown into a kettle of boiling water. Using sound judgment, they immediately jumped out to safety. They needed no focus group or board meeting. Their pain was sharp and instructive. *We better get out now if we want to live,* they might have thought. Nothing like a little hot water to get your attention!

Later, these same amphibians were placed in a kettle of cold water. Some began to notice a slight increase in temperature.

First frog: "I think it's getting hot in here."

Second frog: "You're imagining things. The water is fine."

Third frog: "It's just the air temperature. We're fine."

First frog: "Boy, I could swear it's getting hot, but maybe you're right."

As the story goes, the first frog decided to go along with the crowd. The frogs were oblivious to their peril, to their demise.

Studies seem to indicate that the story of the frogs reveals a good deal of truth about the behavior of living things. Some animals, for example, remain in lethal situations if the danger approaches gradually and insidiously. The key element seems to be the subtle increase in jeopardy as opposed to some glaring and life-threatening attack. And, of course, letting our sound judgment be swayed by others can complicate matters even more!

Puzzling, you say? Yes, this seems to be an unusual phenomenon. Or is it? Are we, at times, like those hapless frogs in a simmering kettle of water, unaware that the heat is being turned up day in and day out, blind to the hazard? Do we sometimes find ways to turn the heat down slightly so that things are tolerable? Resorting to the kinds of mental gymnastics we've already described, we can stay in alarming circumstances for a long time. Far too long!

Our second powerful secret for creating change in your relationship is this: You must *stop making excuses*. Excuses are subtle lies that you have believed to maintain the status quo even though the status quo may be very damaging to your emotional and spiritual health. Men use excuses to keep from changing, and women use them to keep an uneasy (and false) peace. Let's explore how this works and how damaging making excuses is to relationships.

Protecting Our Ego

All of us have developed defenses that we use to protect our egos. None of us want to stare into the face of our vulnerability, our humanity. My own bad behavior in the candy store as a child illustrates the fact that none of us want to admit that we have done something wrong, something for which we might feel embarrassed or ashamed. So, since our creation we have used many different kinds of excuses to make what we are doing seem all right to others. After all, we want their approval. We want to be accepted. So we put on different masks to make ourselves look better than we actually are. We make excuses, and soon we even come to believe those excuses. They are part of the strategy of denial we use to make life less painful.

Let's look back to when we were children. The world was a frightening place. We wanted acceptance more than anything. We wanted to fit in. We needed affirmation, something that may have been in short supply at home. So everything we did was designed, in one way or another, to gain acceptance. Everything we said or did was designed to protect our ego, our sense of self.

Picture a child of six or seven sitting in an overwhelmingly large classroom when suddenly her teacher calls upon her to answer a question. Suddenly, she feels very scared, very small. She hasn't prepared and feels stupid when, in front of the class, she does not know the answer. Embarrassed beyond belief, she can barely hear the teacher ask her why she is not prepared. She fumbles for an answer—any answer that the teacher might accept and that might get her out of this humiliating situation. She sorts through possible explanations, but she knows none is going to work. She is facing a formidable opponent in the teacher, the ultimate authority. Finally, she says that she has not read that part of the book, that she had mistakenly studied another portion. The lie is bold but inadequate. It does not work, and the little girl lowers her head in shame as the teacher scolds her.

We have all used excuses to make troubling situations less uncomfortable. Excuses temporarily deflect the pointing finger of our accuser, whether that accuser is someone on the outside or our own conscience on the inside. We want to get the accuser off our back so that we can enjoy some semblance of peace again. Alexander Solzhenitsyn once said, "We do not err because the truth is difficult to see. It is visible at a glance. We err because it is more comfortable to avoid it."[1]

The science of psychology uses another term for this process. It is called *cognitive dissonance*. It is the uneasiness that we feel when we are doing something that goes against our inner values or when facing the scrutiny of others. For example, let's say that I bought tickets to the Apple Cup game in Pullman, Washington, between Washington State University and the University of Washington. I know the weather will be miserable and the drive treacherous. I go each year only because my brother and I have gone for the last two decades. If you asked me why I would drive four hours to watch a football game, freezing in the nosebleed section of stone-cold bleachers, even though I disliked the experience, I might say that I preferred seeing the game live and enjoying the enthusiasm of the crowd to watching it on television. Though this would not be true, I would feel all right about my decision and get the naysayers off my back. The goal is always to feel a sense of peace within ourselves.

Making excuses for our behavior is common. It is so common that the Scriptures acknowledge that we will struggle with it. Adam and Eve began our struggle with deception, making excuses left and right in an attempt to avoid exposure to the all-seeing God. The Scriptures tell us that our subtle deceptions will create bondage for us, and only the truth will set us free. Sometimes the deceptions will lead us into terribly destructive behavior, perhaps even addictions, but more often deception will simply enable us to avoid change. We won't really expect others to change either. We will be comfortable, but we will be in danger, especially if we are in a troubled relationship.

Cindy and Tim

In a previous chapter, we met Cindy. She is a professional woman who works outside of their home and tries to be a good mother to her three children and a good wife to her husband, Tim. She has many responsibilities and is able to carry them out effectively, at least when her relationship with Tim is going smoothly. When she struggles in her marriage, however, she is in turmoil.

Cindy has been troubled now for some time over her marriage. She has wanted more companionship from Tim for months and has begun wondering if he has formed illicit relationships outside of their marriage. She has no proof of infidelity, but the less affection she receives from him the more her mind wanders. She hungers for an affectionate touch, but the more she wants, the less she gets. She's tried to spice up their relationship by planning special evenings, but Tim acts as though he no longer desires her. She tries not to be bitter, but she occasionally lashes out with accusations that she knows only push Tim further away.

Cindy is fraught with anxiety much of the time. She feels the knot in her stomach, suffers with tension headaches, and worries that she may be getting an ulcer. She is increasingly irritable with the children. She feels impatient and finds that too often she does not want to be bothered with the responsibilities of family life despite what her conscience tells her. She is unable to focus at work and lately has wondered if she can maintain her job. She was unable to meet a deadline for a major project, and she's afraid her boss may be looking to replace her. Her mind is elsewhere, meandering down a path of "what ifs." Her world seems to be spiraling downward, out of control. When I saw her on her next visit, she related what happened when she tried to talk Tim into going with her for counseling from their pastor.

"Tim tells me he is too busy to go and see the pastor, and he would feel awkward talking about our problems with someone he knows so well. He's afraid that word about our relationship would get out, and he wants our problems to remain between us. He also thinks it's too expensive to see a professional counselor and doesn't see why we can't just talk things out ourselves. He always says that I am making mountains out of molehills, and I have to admit that he's not the first person to tell me that. So maybe he's right. Maybe our problems aren't that big. Maybe it's too much to ask for him to go to see our pastor. Maybe he does feel too awkward. Maybe this town is too small. Maybe..."

Self-doubt affects us all. Maybe Tim's arguments are perfectly legitimate. Cindy may turn them over in her mind a hundred times before finally deciding that his arguments are valid. Or will she finally realize that they are all designed to make him and her feel better so that neither of them will have to make any significant changes? Remember, all of these tactics are designed to maintain the status quo. They are designed to protect the all-powerful EGO ("Easing God Out") from having to face unwanted challenges.

Cindy has been hearing excuses and rehearsing them herself for many years. She lives in a world of excuses, lies, and deception. When our world is filled with excuses, we have trouble ferreting out truth from fiction. That is what we must do, however, in order to make our relationships and our lives healthy and happy. And we rely once again on the promise from Scripture that the truth will set us free and that, with God's help, we can be filled with wisdom and understanding. Armed with these tools, we can stop enabling the destructive process to continue and can begin to embark on real change.

When Cindy had finished rationalizing Tim's refusal to attend counseling sessions with their pastor, I told her bluntly that she was merely making excuses for his behavior.

"Tim doesn't want to free up any time to go to counseling. He has plenty of opportunities, but the truth is that he chooses not to give time to something that would threaten him. Tim would feel uncomfortable for a few minutes with the pastor, but maybe that would give way to the kind of comfortable rapport that most people have with their pastor. Tim's fear of word getting out about your problems is unwarranted. The pastor, like other professionals, maintains confidentiality as part of his code of ethics. This is simply another delay and distraction tactic used by Tim to avoid counseling. And truthfully, based on what you've told me about your financial situation, I don't believe this is an expense that your budget could not handle. Tim can always find money for a new set of golf clubs or a new fishing rod, and certainly your marriage is more important than those things. And, finally, he tells you that you are making a mountain out of a molehill. This is simply not true. The demise of your relationship is certainly no molehill. You and Tim both need to get beyond the excuses if you are ever going to see a real change in your marriage."

As Cindy listened to me knock down Tim's excuses, a calm seemed to come over her. She still did not know what she was going to do, but she did know what was true for her. For the moment her thoughts were clear; she had found peace in the midst of her personal storm. She had sought out an advisor who was not inclined to simply give her a pat on the back, who was not afraid to tell her that both she and Tim were out of line. Finally, through her own prayer, quiet reflection, and good counsel, she realized she was doing far too much to excuse Tim's behavior. If change were going to occur, it would have to start with her willingness to demand it.

The Power of Fear

Why would anyone purposely want to keep you off balance? Why would anyone want to manipulate you in order to get you to believe their version of the truth? I believe the answer lies in the power of fear.

Fear paralyzes. Fear has the power to control. Fear demands its own way and does everything in its power to eliminate diverging opinions. Fear causes us to revert back to childish, grasping behaviors, old ways of doing things that provided us with some measure of comfort. But how could fear possess this level of power?

We all fear the loss of control, but perhaps men fear it more than women. They fear their world coming apart and having to deal with things that are threatening to them. Generally speaking, men learn to push painful emotions off the radar screen. Loss, pain, sadness—all are enemies. Men are afraid of facing these and other emotions. Fear pushes all of us out of our comfortable places and into the unknown. We don't want to go to those places.

Tim had constructed a world of secrecy. When Cindy first came to see me, she had no idea what her husband was doing in those secret places. She suspected that they existed, but Tim did everything he could to protect them. He did not want to expose his life to someone like a counselor or pastor who might be critical of what he was doing. He did not want to relinquish control in his relationship. He had constructed myriad excuses to keep Cindy off balance and, most of the time, they worked. The bottom line was that he did not want to have to face parts of himself that inwardly caused fear and shame. So he used denial in massive forms to try to keep his world intact. Cindy had no idea how he could reconcile his behavior with his faith. Maybe his professed commitment to the Lord was as much of a sham as the rest of his life. Sadly, just as Cindy's world was unraveling, so too was Tim's. The more he felt threatened, the more he tried to control her. The more she pushed, the harder he pushed back.

So fear tries vainly to maintain the status quo. We may not like the way things are working out, but we are afraid to face the life of change.

Men Facing Change

In his popular book *Wild at Heart*, John Eldredge wrestles with the issues behind men being men. He describes the fire that burns inside many men, making them bloat like big pufferfish, attempting to create a façade so that no one will poke at them or notice their disguise. They are really little boys inside who don't want to face the truth about themselves. As

Eldredge says, men don't want to face their wounds or their vulnerabilities.

In one passage of the book, Eldredge shares a recurring nightmare. I suppose it is the nightmare of all men in some ways. He tells of spending years in the theater enjoying the accolades that come from life on stage. But he is constantly haunted, perhaps by the shadow side of what all men face.

> I suddenly find myself in a theater—a large, Broadway-style playhouse, the kind every actor aspires to play. The house lights are low and the stage lights full, so from my position onstage I can barely make out the audience, but I sense it is a full house. Standing room only. So far, so good. Actors love playing to a full house. But I am not loving the moment at all. I am paralyzed by fear. A play is under way and I've got a crucial part. But I have no idea what play it is. I don't know my lines; I don't even know my cues....This is man's deepest fear: to be exposed, to be found out, to be discovered as an imposter, and not really a man.[2]

Men facing the prospect that they will feel feeble are often unable to deal effectively with the task at hand, whether that task is finding their way out of the woods when they are lost or finding their way out of marital strife and back to a healthy relationship. Tim doesn't know how to solve the problem, so he puts on his macho attitude with Cindy. He doesn't want to put his ego aside and admit that he is afraid. He does not dare to ask for help and admit that he is lost. He knows how things work: Real men don't show weakness. So he wears the cloak of power and control and uses disguises, threats, and intimidation in the hope they will make his opponent—in his case, his wife—back down. This strategy is often effective. And that is why he continues to use it: It works.

Her Excuses

Just as a man fears confrontations and uses excuses to make his story fit the situation, a woman has her fears too. She too has her excuses that make the situation more palatable. Her vulnerability, however, is much more transparent. She has a lot to lose, and she knows it. Buying his excuses for not changing is easier than changing or looking closely at herself.

I am reminded of another client, Linda, whose husband, Bill, struggled to find his niche in the work world. I watched her battle valiantly to be free from the tyranny of her husband's many excuses for not finding permanent employment. Bill bounced around from job to job, offering random excuses for why he couldn't settle in one place long enough for them to stabilize their family finances. In more than one case, the boss supposedly undermined him. In another, his coworkers didn't respect him. Linda found herself providing for the family. Bill's lack of job stability discouraged, demoralized, and frightened her. She never knew when he might come home and announce once again that he was dissatisfied with his work and wanted to find another job.

Linda found herself fighting nameless, faceless demons. Try as she might to pin Bill down on his chronic pattern of unhappiness, he offered myriad excuses and always promised that his new job would be the last one. But months later she would hear the same set of alibis. He would once again explain that someone else was at fault, someone else did not understand him, and things would be better at the next place of employment.

"Bill doesn't seem to understand how much it's hurt the kids and me to be uprooted. We've left so many schools, houses, and friends that we loved. And all because of Bill's problems."

Gradually, Linda lost respect for Bill. At first she sympathized with his plight. She had a steady job that helped provide ballast for their listing vessel. She could "carry him" and was happy to do so. But as time went on and one unhappy job led to another, she grew more restless. She faced the task of believing him or confronting him about his obviously irresponsible patterns. When confronted, he always had an excuse, a reason that things did not work out. Years passed, and her affections for him declined along with her respect. Still, she persisted in hoping that things would change. Her fears stood between her and her desire to scream. But what did she fear?

When Linda first came to me, she refused to dig beneath the surface and examine Bill's excuses. If she were to truly see things the way they were, look dead-on at the ugly pattern that Bill had established for himself, she would be forced to change. She would have to take a stand or make some internal change so that she could live with this personality trait. Living with the instability of his job choices was intolerable to her. That left her with a single course of action: taking a stand, facing her fears, and making some tough decisions. And that meant facing her fears of raising the children alone and managing the meager budget by herself. It also meant coming face-to-face with her own vulnerability and her powerful desire to have a man to lean on.

What if Bill refused to get help? What if Bill refused to change? How would she support herself and her two young children? What if she was wrong, and Bill really wasn't at fault? Life looked terribly frightening, and her world seemed ready to crash down around her. Yet to do nothing meant living in a world of lingering insecurity and marital demise. She had bought his excuses for years, and nothing had changed. She had rationalized the problem for years, and nothing had changed. She had prayed, been patient, and been a dutiful wife for years, and nothing had changed. She decided that doing nothing but waiting for change was not the right course for her. After several sessions, she understood that she had to take action.

His Excuses

For each of her impatient questions, Bill had a ready response, an excuse for any situation. At times they seemed so believable. She was confused. Could she be wrong about him?

Linda knew in her heart that Bill was not a bad person. If he were, leaving him would be easier. But Bill was a wonderful man in many ways. He was a doting father, and their children loved him. He was kind and generous. Everyone in their church liked his charm and contagious smile.

His manner with Linda was not aggressive. He did not bully her or intimidate her. His manner was soft-spoken and disarming. He had big blue eyes that screamed for compassion. He pleaded that he could not help what was happening to him. He was the victim of unfortunate circumstances. He tried to make the jobs work but became dissatisfied after a while. He was envious of Linda and her "luck" in finding just the right job.

"It took me a long time to admit it," Linda said, "but now I realize that Bill has always been this way. Even in high school, nothing was ever his fault. I suppose for a while I really did believe that he was a victim of sorts. But I can't ignore it anymore. I have waited so long for him to finally grow up and be a man, but he is the same little boy he always was."

Bill and Linda had a dance that they had done for years that was quite destructive. The dance, with choreographed movements on both parts, looked like this: Linda...

- scolds
- challenges
- cries
- attacks
- gives up
- feels confused and guilty

Meanwhile, Bill...

- whines
- cries
- protests
- complains
- walks away

Ultimately, Linda lost her voice in the fog of excuses. Bill worked long and hard to play the victim and get Linda to believe that he could not help his circumstances. He is merely the unfortunate actor in a bad play. He cannot help what is happening to him. Instead, it is the company's fault, the economy's fault, his parents' fault, his school's fault. Faced with his myriad excuses and her desire to keep their family together, Linda relinquishes power. As a result, no change can possibly occur.

Separating Wheat from Chaff

The world of the farmer calls for a discerning eye and plenty of patience. The farmer looks out over his crops dispassionately and makes critical decisions about when to water, when to fertilize, when to prune. He decides when to harvest and how to save the nutritious product from the waste. He is capable of separating the wheat from the chaff. His implacable nerve comes with experience.

I do not pretend to know much about the farmer's world, but I have watched the orchardist snip and cut in masterful surgeon-like moves to enhance the fruit of the following season. What appeared to me to be destructive action proved later to bring an unexpected bounty.

In the Gospel of John, the Lord says that He is the master gardener. "He cuts off every branch in me that bears no fruit, while every branch that does bear fruit he prunes so that it will be even more fruitful" (John 15:2).

The process of deciphering truth from fiction is similar to the process of pruning. Separating fact from excuses. The critical eye can see what is the truth and what masquerades as truth. For change to occur we must discover, acknowledge, and own the truth. Partners in marriage must be willing to identify the truth and (perhaps painfully) deal with it. Effective change cannot occur unless the truth is first separated from fiction.

Knowing and Telling the Truth

Admitting and telling the truth is not as easy as it sounds. We would all like to believe that we are truth-tellers, but most of us gloss over the truth as often as we are able. We use excuses and alibis to avoid being responsible for our actions. We hide from the truth as long as those around us will allow us. And that is where you come in. Your part is to look and listen, to know and tell the truth. The truth is often painful, but it is the only path to freedom.

In the wonderful book *Women's Ways of Knowing,* the authors discuss the difficulty women face in "claiming the power of their mind." The authors suggest that our culture encourages women to listen to other voices and thus lose the power of their own voice. They have been taught to listen without question to the voices of their husbands and other authorities, and this can be a dangerous proposition.

> The extreme sex-role stereotypes that the silent women accept reflect the powerlessness they have experienced. Men are active and get things done, while women are passive and incompetent. This view undoubtedly helps the women make sense of their own dependence and deference to authorities.[3]

I am not questioning the godly authority of the husband. But we must not confuse godly authority with ego-centered power and control. We must not mistake truth for a dogmatic position that stifles another voice. And women must never lose their own inspired thinking abilities.

Again, I encourage you to face what you know to be the truth, embrace it, and then speak it. Speak the truth in love, but speak it. Just as you do not sit still for alibis and arguments from your children, do not abide them from your husband. Clearly state what you believe is happening and be prepared to take action.

Linda finally was no longer willing to accept Bill's excuses. After nearly a year of counseling, she was finally ready to make a change.

"I watched Bill's patterns with employment over the years. He had ten jobs in seven years. It took guts, but I finally admitted that this pattern is unfair to the children and intolerable for me. He had always blamed his lack of advancement on the boss, the company, or someone else. I think it's time for him to take responsibility for his struggles. I am willing to look at my part in this pattern of events and how I enable things to keep going the way they are. But I do not intend to continue living like this for the rest of my life. I have carefully thought it through, and I want us to see the pastor and a marriage counselor to end this horrible pattern of financial instability. I want us to be accountable to others in our lives."

To many, Linda's blunt assessment of her husband's behavior may sound harsh and uncaring. But this situation begs for honesty. It is just waiting for someone to clear the fog and declare a course of action. Telling the truth is not uncaring but rather the most considerate and compassionate thing you can do. It offers hope for change rather than con- ceding to being stuck. You are capable of repairing damages and moving forward. But first, you must get past the excuses. And the only way to begin the process is to tell yourself it must be done.

Four

The Inner Vow of Silence

*No man is an island entire of itself;
every man is a piece of the continent,
a part of the main.*

JOHN DONNE

I have a hand-scrawled note taped to my desk at work to help me keep things in perspective. It reads: "You would worry a lot less about what people think about you if you knew how seldom they do."

That quotation gives me both peace and pause. I am comforted by the fact that people are probably not out there gossiping about David Hawkins' most recent embarrassment. Heaven knows I do not need anyone clamoring about what a fool I have made of myself. I am quite able to reveal my own foolishness.

The quote also creates tension for me because I would like to believe that I am on my friends' minds and in their hearts. I want to imagine that they are taking time from their busy lives to wonder about me, pray for me, and wish me well. The most terrible loneliness comes when we are in a difficult trial and no one shares the burden.

Curiously, however, our loneliness is often self-imposed. How quickly we can build a moat around our castle so that no one may enter. We quite naturally and comfortably withdraw into an inner world of silence. In the dark places of the soul, we brood. And we fester. And...well, you know what we do. Our problems grow larger and larger, and we feel less and less capable of solving them on our own. Before long, we see ourselves as Atlas, carrying the weight of the world on our shoulders. No wonder we often appear slumped-over and downcast. Our bodies broadcast the messages of our souls.

Perhaps this book finds you in a lonely place, hunkered down and telling yourself, *The problem is all in my head.* Perhaps your partner has suggested the same thing. If only the problem were that simple. In the midst of your loneliness you will find help from our third powerful secret: learning to *break the inner vow of silence.*

Holly and Jeff

Holly and Jeff have been married for nearly eight years. They enjoyed a wonderful courtship, and the early years of their marriage were exciting, productive, and rewarding. Both have careers that are emotionally and financially satisfying. Lately, however, the pressures of two careers have taken their toll. Collisions between them began to occur with greater frequency, and that led Holly to seek counsel from me.

Holly had been in the advertising business for nearly ten years and was a formidable opponent when negotiating new contracts for the firm. She was recognized for her deft verbal skills, quick wit, and no-nonsense way of handling problems. Her steel blue eyes could cut a swath through a boardroom door. Holly recognized her strength in the business world, but she was frustrated that she could not seem to negotiate as well with her husband. More and more frequently, she found herself withdrawing into silence and carrying a grudge after even the most minor confrontation.

Holly had always loved Jeff. They were high school sweethearts and married after graduation. He worked as a contractor and sometimes felt inferior to her "high-gloss business life," but they enjoyed their life together. Holly was delighted to join Jeff in building a country home to escape the pressures of city life. They had designed the home together and had similar tastes in decorating. Raising and breeding golden retrievers was another pastime they shared. Life was fine until the children arrived. Then things changed dramatically. She shared her story with me during one of her earlier counseling sessions.

"After we had the two little guys I noticed that Jeff put more pressure on me to be home. He resented my long hours at the office, and I understand that. I've worked hard to pare down my schedule and am now home most evenings. But that isn't good enough for him. He constantly chides me to quit my job and be a stay-at-home mother. But that is not me. He simply will not quit bothering me about it. I try to negotiate with him, but it's his way or no way."

Holly paused. "I'm not sure that I even need to be here. I almost cancelled. We're doing okay, I suppose. I just need to learn to live with his outbursts. I know he's not keen on seeing a counselor. He went once before but didn't like the guy."

"So, Holly," I said, "why are you here? If things are fine, why did you make this appointment? I suspect that you try to talk yourself into believing that life is tolerable, and then it all comes crumbling around your ears. Am I right?"

Holly began to cry. She looked at me for several moments, dabbing at her eyes.

"I can't live like this any longer. He tries to control my life, and even worse, he won't talk to me about it. He tells me how things are going to be. I think he is threatened by my job. I am not sure why, but he is. The more threatened he becomes, the more he wants to tell me how our house should be run. He now tells me how the laundry should be done, when dinner should be ready, what we should eat, and even how it should be prepared. I can't stand it."

"So what do you do about it?"

"I guess I complain. And then I don't say anything. There is no use talking to Jeff. He doesn't talk. He lectures. I've learned to keep my mouth shut."

"So you complain and then drop it. You let the tension build and then, finally, you are ready to come apart."

"Yes, I guess that is what happens."

"Is that working for you?"

"No, I guess not. No, not at all, actually."

"I see why you are reluctant to confront him. At this point, talking to Jeff only gives him more targets to shoot at. I suspect that whenever you offer him some reasons why work is meaningful to you, he just shoots them down."

"Exactly. He answers that we can make it on his salary and the boys need me at home. He feels like it's his job to be the major breadwinner in the home."

"Are you ready to stir the waters? I'm not talking about striking up arguments with him at every turn, but you need to be very clear about what is important to you and have some fairly direct conversations about that."

"That all sounds great, but he won't listen to me."

"That is where I come in. Change requires intervention. You can't do the same old thing and expect different results. You have to do things differently. He needs to come in for counseling and look at the way you two talk to each other. Are you ready to rock the boat?"

"Should we have him join us next time?"

"No, you have some work to do before you are ready to negotiate with him. I want you to focus on several steps. They may seem a bit silly, but trust me. They will be important building blocks for our upcoming sessions with Jeff. First, write out why things must change.

• What is wrong with the way things are now?

- Can you live this way if nothing changes?
- What are you doing that keeps things the same?
- How do you feel about rocking the boat?
- Can you live with tension while we change the way you talk to one another?"

You may wonder about my game plan. I wanted Holly to work on several important issues that are consistent themes in this book. Perhaps you will be able to identify with them.

Holly needed to examine her own feelings. She was uncertain a real problem existed. Jeff had succeeded in getting her to question her motives and actions.

Holly needed to become crystal clear about why she was unhappy and realize that those feelings would not just disappear. Inaction on her part would lead to more of the same: more misery, more destructive patterns of relating.

Holly needed to prepare for the disequilibrium that occurs during change. Her boat would rock, and she needed to prepare for that.

Finally, Holly needed to think about her part in the ongoing destructive patterns. Hiding behind a veil of silence kept her peaceful for brief moments but did nothing to heal her deep wounds or the problems in her marriage. I ended the session with Holly by encouraging her to be assertive. I never assume for a moment that coming to a counseling session is easy. Making changes in long-standing patterns of relating is a tremendous challenge.

"It must have taken a lot of courage to come in for counseling knowing that Jeff doesn't really believe in it. You're in a lot of pain, but you have told me and yourself that you really want things to change. You've taken a big first step."

Patterns of Communication

The renowned and innovative family counselor and researcher Virginia Satir made a number of profound discoveries about the ways families relate. Her observations and conclusions have led to accepted practices among counselors and psychologists today.

Satir watched countless families and marriage partners interact. She noted that "communication is the greatest single factor affecting a person's health and his relationship to others."[1] She found that people have ingenious ways of avoiding honest communication. Among other tactics, she found that people often use...

- placating so the other person won't get angry
- blaming so the other person will regard you as strong and not responsible
- computing, using big words so you will think the threat is harmless and you are powerful
- distracting by ignoring the threat and behaving as if it were not there

Which patterns may fit your marital relationship? Do you or your partner tend to blame others as a means of getting yourselves off the hook? Has your partner refused to accept responsibility when he has done something wrong? Do either of you withdraw into silence?

Healthy couples and families are able to do several critical things, according to Satir. They are able to...

- see what they see, and be affirmed for it
- feel what they feel, and share those feelings openly
- think what they think, and not be criticized for it

If you are not free to do those three things, you will feel unsafe to be who you are. You may feel the need to withdraw. But now is the time to break the inner vow of silence and affirm what you see, think, and feel.

Ending the Isolation

Holly is similar to many people in relationships that aren't working. They keep their struggles a secret behind closed doors for years before venturing out for help. By that time, the problem has often increased to an unbearable level. It has congealed and become cancerous with tentacles reaching into many other parts of the relationship. In such cases, trying to solve our own problems is like trying to perform surgery on ourselves. Generally inadvisable!

Hiding in isolation does not end with simply "suffering in silence." The impact of maintaining this vow to bear your grief internally can have serious ramifications.

You may need to break a faulty inner vow. Early in life, we make decisions that are destructive, and then we live by them until we hit a crisis. Often we are not even aware we have made the decision, but we continue following it down a long, destructive path. We are usually unaware other paths even exist.

Holly made an inner vow to keep her struggle quiet. She felt ashamed for complaining. After all, her husband was hardworking, diligent, and devout. Jeff's arguments seemed sound and inarguable. She decided something must be wrong with her—*that* must be why she was so exhausted and frustrated. So she made a vow to change herself somehow in an attempt to cope with the way things were. She vowed not to talk to her friends or pastor about her struggles. She would not bring shame to her marriage by coming out with the problem. But such a vow, not analyzed, makes change impossible.

Silence prevents you from examining the problem from other angles. Silence keeps you enmeshed with the problem, going over the same old twisted facts again and again. No new information can emerge when past vows are unbreakable.

As a Christian psychologist, I believe strongly that we need to examine our problems from new angles and base our decisions on biblical principles, such as the authority of the

Scriptures in our lives. How easily we get caught up in vicious circles in our minds. When this occurs, we put ourselves at a disadvantage: We do not have the luxury of wisdom from our elders, Christian friends, pastor, or counselor. We are left to rehearse the problem again and again with little hope of new thinking or real change.

Consider how small your world becomes when you maintain the vow of silence. It is like a box with no windows, and living in it makes you vulnerable to feelings of profound discouragement and depression. But you can invite someone to walk alongside to open windows, let in a breath of fresh air, and point out possibilities that you had not considered. You need a larger space than your own heart to reflect on the problem and its solutions.

Silence keeps you from finding support. We all need help dealing with our troubles. The Scriptures are replete with examples of people who leaned on one another during difficult times. In fact, the apostle Paul admonishes us to "carry each other's burdens, and in this way you will fulfill the law of Christ" (Galatians 6:2). We simply cannot carry some burdens by ourselves. Many emotional struggles fit into this category, such as grieving the death of a loved one, feeling betrayed, and dealing with interpersonal conflicts.

Thankfully, many churches have risen to the occasion and developed support groups for divorced people, singles, mothers of preschoolers, and more.

Silence keeps you self-absorbed. Self-absorbed people do not listen to others but rather rehearse their own tale of woe. When we do not hold problems up to the light for examination, they tend to grow in the dark. These problems become overwhelming and can easily lead to depression. We need to actively read good material on the topic of our concern, listen to good teaching, talk to supportive friends and counsel, and read what the Scriptures have to say on the issue.

The Critical Voice of Shame

Some words hurt, and some hurt deeply. Perhaps worst of all are words that keep on hurting for a long time. Those words are poisoned with shame. But what is shame, exactly?

John Bradshaw pioneered our current understanding about this sticky emotion in his groundbreaking book, *Healing the Shame That Binds You.*

> Shame as a healthy human emotion can be transformed into shame as a state of being. As a state of being, shame takes over one's whole identity. To have shame as an identity is to believe that one's being is flawed, that one is defective as a human being. Once shame is transformed into an identity, it becomes toxic and dehumanizing.[2]

Bradshaw goes on to detail the ravaging effects of shame. He says that once we feel that our true self is defective and flawed, we go to great lengths to replace it with a false self. This is the self that we present to the world. We go into hiding, sometimes in a very literal sense. We take on a vow of silence, knowing that to speak means to risk ridicule. We do not want others to see what we are hiding. Bradshaw says that once we take on this false self to hide our shameful parts, we cease to exist psychologically. At that moment we are no longer an authentic human being.

For Holly, shame means that she does not want others to know she is having marital problems. After all, her husband is a prominent person in the church. Others look to him for counsel and guidance. The pastor relies on him for leadership. People expect him to be able to manage his home. Those expectations can become twisted when we expect anyone to be perfect. Holly is proud of Jeff's position. This pride has become part of her "false self," part of her identity. Admitting that even leaders in the church have dysfunctional marriages would rock her boat. Much of the larger church participates in this vow of secrecy, and it desperately needs our assistance in breaking the destructive silence.

Bradshaw believes that shame is the core and consequence of Adam's fall and thus the fall of all humankind. Adam failed to accept who he was, to acknowledge his true identity. He wanted to be more than he was, to be without his essential limitations, to be equivalent to God. He wanted to be more than human. In his pride, Adam desired a false self that led to his destruction. Adam alienated his true self and then went into hiding. Have you alienated parts of yourself, wanting to be more, trying to separate yourself from your essential limitations? Or have you too willingly decided that wanting to improve your relationship was the very sign of pride that caused Adam's fall? The key is finding a balance between the need to take responsibility for your life and the need to submit to God's will.

You remember that Adam and Eve tried to become like God, knew that they had committed a heinous crime, and went into hiding. God had to search them out, for they were ashamed (Genesis 3:9-10). Once they chose to become other than what God created them to be, they became naked and humiliated.

As I sat with Holly, I could sense that she was holding a great deal of emotion inside. She spoke of her growing weariness with her marriage, her headaches, and her gnawing dissatisfaction with her job. But she could see no solutions.

Holly's Silence

I asked Holly to describe "walking on pins and needles" around Jeff, and living with his critical attitude about her desire to have a career.

"Jeff lets me know subtly as well as directly that I should be doing things differently. He reminds me of how blessed we are to have two wonderful sons, to have a great church, and to have opportunities in ministry. He reminds me of how blessed we are financially. He even cites Scripture to support his position that I should not be working the hours I work, or even working at all. He speaks with a voice of authority. How can I argue against that? But I have this nagging feeling that we should be able to talk about this issue, to negotiate an agreement that works for both of us."

Holly paused for a moment to grab some tissue from her purse. She wiped her eyes.

"But no matter what Jeff says, I'm not happy with the way things are. I do not feel blessed. I feel tired. I feel misunderstood. I don't think Jeff has a clue how much this is bothering me. He listens, but I don't think he knows how troubled I am by his criticism."

"I understand your frustration," I said. "You enjoy your work, and it is important to you. However, I think the bigger issue is that you and Jeff have not been able to work out a solution that fits your marriage and family. I am concerned about your lack of communication with one another. That is what I really think needs work.

"More importantly," I continued, "you are not being honest with Jeff. You stop short of telling him exactly what you think or at least what you are really feeling. You have never sat down and told him how disappointed and angry you are with him. And I doubt that you have ever listened truly to how frustrated he is. Perhaps if he were here he would say that he feels misunderstood as well."

I paused to let what I had said sink in. Would she rail against me, or would she consider that she needed to change the way she related to Jeff? Would she see that she was living a lie and needed to come out of hiding? Her pattern of retreating into silence and later blowing up was not working. That only created more shame for her.

Healing the Shame That Binds You

Shame did not originate with Holly and Jeff or with you and me. It has been around for a long, long time. But we were not created in shame: "The man and his wife were both naked, and they felt no shame" (Genesis 2:25). Sadly, that came to a screeching halt a short time later, but through Jesus we can find relief from that troubling emotion. "There is now no condemnation for those who are in Christ Jesus" (Romans 8:1).

These words are certainly true, but they do not erase the effects of shame that we carry because of our actions. We must apply certain principles to receive the healing balm that rids us of shame.

Supportive Relationships

Healing starts with a critical first step, which is to come out of hiding and break the inner vow of silence. Coming out of hiding is a powerful beginning. We must build an interpersonal bridge to others so that they can discover who we are and what we are afraid to talk about.

Consider how many times you have held on to negative feelings because you were afraid no one would understand. Yet we are all created alike. I may not have traveled the same road as you, but I have experienced loss, shame, humiliation, and remorse. Are those not many of the feelings that you also keep to yourself? Do we not share the same general emotional makeup? We have enough in common to relate to one another, but only if we take the time and effort.

You need a situation that helps you feel comfortable sharing what is happening. You must find people who will not humiliate you for what you are experiencing. This may take some doing. In the end, however, you will know who can be trusted.

Bradshaw provides additional advice on this topic. "Since it was personal relationships that set up our toxic shame, we need personal relationships to heal our shame. This is crucial. We must risk reaching out and looking for nonshaming relationships if we are to heal our shame."[3] We need one another to heal. We need to belong to a loving community to heal. We need to feel validated. We need to know that we are not crazy for what we are seeing, hearing, and experiencing. We need a place where we can grieve, letting the tears flow for as long as necessary.

At times, we can find this healing community in the church. At times, sadly, we cannot. The church includes all kinds of people, all on their own journeys toward Christ-likeness. Sanctimonious, judgmental people will thwart the efforts of a recovering person.

Reaching Out to God

In addition to finding a base of support where we can tell it like it is, we need to reach out to God. God can help us restore the four relationships damaged by Adam: the relationship with God, the relationship with self, the relationship with brother and neighbor, and the relationship with nature. We must step outside of ourselves, come out of hiding, and seek the face of God. We must humbly admit that we are not perfect, realize that we have emotions that are powerful and painful, and seek guidance on how to deal with these complicated feelings. We can no longer rely only upon ourselves. The time comes when we need a friend, pastor, or counselor who can provide a fresh perspective and caring advice.

In the book of Proverbs we read that wisdom is granted to all that seek it. We have this great promise:

> If you accept my words and store up my commands within you, turning your ear to wisdom and applying your heart to understanding, and if you call out for insight and cry aloud for understanding, and if you look for it as for silver and search for it as for hidden treasure, then you will understand the fear of the LORD and find the knowledge of God (Proverbs 2:1-5).

Honesty with Ourselves

Another step in healing is to be honest with ourselves. We must admit that life is sometimes unmanageable and that we do not have all the answers. Holly had walled off critical parts of herself so that she could be at peace. But her efforts did not work because she was not truly being honest with herself. We should never be so naïve as to believe that prayer can solve our problems if we are unwilling to commit ourselves to action. Holly wanted to present a certain image to the public, her husband, and God, but inside she was miserable. She wanted to dis-member herself by putting away the uncomfortable parts of her life. Instead, she needed to re-member her pain and confront it.

Holly needs to be honest with herself. She is miserable and harbors deep feelings of resentment toward her husband. Keeping him out of the loop of her feelings does no one any good. Telling herself that she should not feel this way denies what she is experiencing and makes change impossible.

King David is well-known for honestly crying out about his feelings. "I remembered you, O God, and I groaned; I mused, and my spirit grew faint. You kept my eyes from closing; I was too troubled to speak" (Psalm 77:3-4). He complained repeatedly about his situation and at times lived in a self-created world of isolation. But he continued to plead to the Lord for comfort, all the while attempting to break out of his debilitating loneliness.

Integration

A last step in healing from toxic shame is integrating our shame-based, disowned parts. In the final analysis, healthy shame comes with the understanding that we all make mistakes and are fallible. We are not God! Look in the mirror and say, straight out, that you are flawed. Mature people can acknowledge mistakes, learn from them, and yet not let those mistakes get them down.

As you consider this deep healing work, remember what the Psalmist says about the heart of God toward us:

> For you created my inmost being; you knit me together in my mother's womb. I praise you because I am fearfully and wonderfully made; your works are wonderful, I know that full well. My frame was not hidden from you when I was made in the secret place. When I was woven together in the depths of the earth, your eyes saw my unformed body (Psalm 139:13-16).

David says that we are "fearfully and wonderfully made," and I have to believe that he was referring to all of our components, not just the nice ones. God knows all of the parts, even the ones that cause us shame. He accepts those parts, as well. And we can risk opening ourselves to Him. Make friends with these divided parts of yourself. But never forget that putting those pieces back together under the mantle of personal well-being is your ultimate goal.

What Makes Him Tick?

We have spent much of this chapter peering into the lives of Jeff and Holly. This modern-day, dual-income couple is quite typical of many married couples today. They face the pressure of trying to manage two jobs, two incomes, and two children. It is a daunting task.

Like most who attempt this balancing act, they have not been successful, though hope is on the horizon. The month after I met with Holly, Jeff agreed to seek help and find better ways to talk about emotionally loaded issues. If he had not been willing, the prognosis would have been much bleaker. Together they have begun the process of learning new ways of communicating.

But what do you suppose might be going on inside Jeff? As you may guess, seeing his wife in the glittery business world is threatening for Jeff, especially when he is stuck with the dirty job of hammering nails. He fears losing his wife to some high-tech executive though her faithfulness to him has never waned. He also wants her to be home for their children. He came from a "traditional" family where his mother was home for him and his siblings. He wants the same for his kids.

Another piece to this puzzle has to do with control. He would be reluctant to admit it, but Jeff wants complete command. Because Holly is an intelligent, independent woman, he feels his authority as "the man of the house" slipping away. He knew going in to this marriage that Holly was a career woman, but he did not anticipate the pressures involved. The more she resists his urgings, the more he feels the loss of control. Sadly, he has fought this battle by using controlling tactics that were destined to fail.

Ultimately, the only tactic that will work is for both to truly listen to one another. They must set their agendas aside and work toward a solution in which both will be satisfied. They must seek the elusive "win-win" situation. And they will find it if they loosen their grip and let go of the power struggle. They are willing to work toward that end, so there is hope.

Now What?

We seem to know intuitively that we must share ourselves with others. We must talk about what is bothering us and reveal the stirrings in our souls. We hunger for special places and people that help us give birth to those deep inner stirrings. We don't want to be silenced. We are simply trying to live out loud.

Tragically, we often make unconscious agreements to keep the silence. The vow is bound by shame, and the silence kills the struggling spirit.

Our task is to break the inner vow of silence. To be brave enough to be ourselves even if that means facing conflict. To champion those gifts that we have been granted and give one another enough room to live honest lives. This is no small undertaking in a world that clamors for conformity, insisting that we not rock the boat.

But before you can expect others to understand and accept you, you must first honor and respect your own feelings and point of view. You must understand and accept yourself. Once you accomplish this, you will develop the courage to reach out to others for support and understanding. And in most cases, you will get it.

Five

Real Change
Requires Real Action

Things do not change, we do.

HENRY DAVID THOREAU

Patricia came to my office on a dull, gray winter morning. The weatherman had predicted snow, but none came. The weather seemed to match Patricia's mood: a foreboding emptiness pregnant with threats.

Patricia was a 24-year-old with a promising career as a claims adjuster for a large insurance company, and she appeared destined for an executive position. Normally a woman of decisive action and razor-sharp wit, she seemed especially cautious when she came to my office to talk about her relationship with Greg.

Two years ago, Patricia had fallen in love with a man whom she saw as charismatic, sensitive, and strikingly handsome. I suspect she saw him riding a splendid white steed as well. Greg was gallant, caring, and kind. She had been dating for some time and was ready for an exclusive, committed relationship. In Greg, Patricia saw the potential for a match made in heaven.

As time went by, their relationship grew stronger. They shared a love of outdoor activities, an appreciation for the arts, and similar spiritual values. They seemed to be in sync on life's most important issues.

Everything was wonderful in their new relationship except for one small but frustrating thing: Greg had a habit of spending money on his "toys." He occasionally made large purchases and acted as if they were no big deal. He placed the purchases on credit cards, reassuring Patricia that he always made the payments in a timely manner. She gleaned from their conversations, however, that he had maxed out two cards. She saw the debt mounting and wondered if he would always be able to pay it off. She thought the exorbitant interest rates were a foolish waste of money.

As she watched this process, she wondered if anything was truly wrong with it. He liked to buy hi-tech stereo components, computer equipment, and gadgets for his car. Clearly, he felt entitled to make the purchases because he had a right to use his money as he pleased. After all, they were not married, and he assured her that things would change when they were. She was not so sure. She wondered if he would have the discipline necessary to save for a house and other larger expenses.

Patricia watched Greg and saw that he spent nearly all of his expendable income on toys and worried that this would become a source of tension between them. She saved some money each month and spent anything that was left over cautiously. She liked to splurge occasionally but tended to be more of a saver than Greg.

Patricia spoke to Greg about her concerns, but he responded with significant defensiveness. He wondered why she was so preoccupied with this issue. He was able to make all of his payments and had never filed for bankruptcy. He accused her of overreaction and wanted her to trust him to keep out of financial trouble.

At first, she overlooked Greg's spending habits, and they seemed to literally dance around the issue. Wonderful dinners, ballroom dancing, and other gala events filled their time. Their eyes sparkled when they saw one another. They laughed long and loudly together. But she could never get beyond the underlying tension about finances and the effect they might eventually have on their relationship. Any attempts to let go of the problem seemed futile. At times she wondered if she were making too big of a deal of this problem. Everything else was wonderful, so she wondered why this issue should bother her. She was in love with him. She wanted nothing to put a damper on those wonderful feelings. But as we have learned, if something feels like a big issue, it may be a big issue.

Ambivalence

After their initial argument about the problem, Patricia fretted for months about bringing it up again. She felt an intense ambivalence about mentioning such a sensitive topic. She knew that he would be defensive about the issue. Clearly he did not see any problem, and he gave her the distinct message that the topic was off-limits. She watched as he ran up charges on his credit cards, and she bit her tongue to avoid annoying him. Ever so slowly they built a barrier of unexpressed concerns. The issue had expanded from his spending to their inability to talk about his spending. A bigger problem was developing.

Patricia held on to her resentment for months. She tried to push the problem down, but it kept sneaking back up to the surface. She was usually able to tell herself that the positives of the relationship far outweighed the negatives. Perhaps that was true. She dreamed of a long life with Greg, free from any concerns about his credit cards and lack of responsibility. Denial worked fine for a while. But finally she admitted to herself that any problem they experienced now was only likely to get worse, not better. She had some difficult decisions to make.

Patricia needed to do some soul-searching. How important was the issue of Greg's spending? How serious was his refusal to really talk about it? If he did agree to work on the problem, which he hadn't, what were the chances of real change? Now she needed to grab hold of our fourth powerful secret: *Real change requires real action!*

Real Change Requires Real Action

Change does not just happen. We all know this—or do we? Do we realistically assess the difficulty of making fundamental changes? Unfortunately, most of us dance around issues. We don't want to take decisive action, for doing so requires that we endure some discomfort. Change means we will no longer be able to live in our familiar ruts. We will have to deal with anxiety, apprehension, and perhaps even fear. Most of us would rather circle around problems than grapple with those feelings.

What should Patricia do? Does she allow something as seemingly inconsequential as Greg's spending to damage their flourishing relationship? Is his overspending a petty matter or something that requires her to take action? And what of their inability to talk directly about the problem? Was that a more substantial matter?

When Patricia was honest with herself, she realized that her feelings about Greg's spending ran deep. The issue was trivial on one level, yet on another it needled her. She could not help noticing his eyes widen when they passed a stereo store. And every time they passed a computer store, he invariably asked if they could go in for just a minute, which turned into half an hour. She wondered if his spending was a sign of weakness in his character, a lack of discipline that would affect their life together for years to come.

As I worked with Patricia, I encouraged her to voice all of the issues related to spending. She had to come to terms with several important truths. First, she had to decide how important Greg's spending habits were to her. Some purchases might be small matters that should be overlooked in light of the many positive aspects of the relationship. Other expenditures might point to future problems and require immediate attention. Ultimately, she had to decide.

Assuming that Patricia decides Greg's spending is a worthy matter for concern, she must come to terms with the challenge of change. Change is difficult under the best of conditions. Ignoring problems never solves anything; in fact, they usually get worse over time.

Too often we assume that the things we want and need from a relationship will come to us.

- If we ask for something, it will come.
- Our partner will want to please us.
- He or she will be willing to make the changes necessary to please us.
- If our partner makes an effort, change will occur.
- He or she knows what we need and will work at meeting the need.

But reality is a bit harsher.

- Most people are self-absorbed.
- They are concerned mostly about their own well-being.
- They cannot read our minds.
- They may want to change but may not be motivated enough to do so.
- They have not fully calculated the requirements for change.

- They have not had a serious discussion with their partner about this.

Both parties often have an unrealistic appraisal of the situation. In most cases, the situation is far more serious than either has realized. Change does *not* just happen. Many ingredients are necessary for change to occur. Abandoning long-standing spending habits, for example, requires altering an ingrained character trait. This is far different from learning to take out the garbage.

Collusion

Sadly, many couples play a game of collusion with one another. They talk about the problem, bicker about the problem, protest the injustice of the problem, but never truly address the severity of the problem.

You have undoubtedly heard of the "stinky elephant in the room" syndrome. This syndrome occurs in most relationships. The partners silently agree to never really address an issue that is troubling them. This does not mean that they never talk about the problem. They just silently agree to never seriously address it at the depth necessary to resolve it.

Consider your current relationship. Can you honestly say that you take the following steps to resolve a sticky matter?

- Make time to talk about an issue.
- Stretch yourself to be candid.
- Own your part in the problem.
- Stay with the conversation until resolution is found.
- Hold each other accountable for change.

Most people do not rigorously apply themselves to talking about the stinky elephants in the room and, consequently, spend far too much time stepping carefully around messy piles.

Unless couples acknowledge the smell for what it is, they become quite adept at pretending that no problem exists. After all, who wants to come home every evening after work to face dirty dishes in the sink and laundry that needs to be done, and then take on the big, stinky elephant waiting in the living room?

The temporary solution for most couples is to make the pact of collusion. It goes like this:

> I'll agree not to talk about this sticky, stinky matter if you will. We'll pretend together that change will just happen, and we both will be happy some day. In the meantime, let's do whatever is necessary to avoid the topic.

And so it goes. Avoidance, denial, rationalization. We make every effort to dodge the dreaded, painful conversation about how serious things are and how difficult change is.

Only when we finally face the awful truth is change possible. In every relational difficulty, both parties must acknowledge their part in the collusive dance. Both must be willing to eradicate shame, blame, and denial from their relational patterns.

I recently worked with a couple, married for more than 15 years, who came to see me because they had been dancing around the problem of sexual unhappiness for many years. They could not even remember what had led up to the separate sleeping arrangement. A fight here, an icy week there. Slowly but surely they had begun a pattern of sleeping in separate bedrooms. They would kiss one another goodnight and head off to separate bedrooms. Neither was willing to ask why they were living this way.

Collusion worked for this couple until he decided that the problem needed to be addressed. As with most problems, it had been gnawing away at him. He wondered if she was as frustrated as he was, but he had been fearful of her reaction. He was pleasantly surprised when she acknowledged that the situation had been bothering her as well, and they agreed to do something about it. They overcame a huge hurdle by simply talking about the problem in an open and honest way. They seemed to grasp that real change requires real action. They now are working diligently on their problem and making steady progress.

Resistance to Change

Before we can even think about taking on the daunting task of change, we must first admit that we naturally do not fully commit to change. This is an imposing tendency that we must face directly before we can tackle the problems that confront us.

I recall a conversation with my oldest son when he was at the height of adolescence. He was literally changing daily before my eyes. Early one evening he asked me to sit down and talk. For a teenager, just taking that step is incredibly difficult. I knew something powerful must be coming.

"Dad," he said, "it seems like you don't really like me. You always notice the things I do wrong and never notice when I do things right. You don't want me to have fun. You just want me to work hard like you, but I don't want to be just like you. I'm different from you. I wish you'd realize that, and I wish you'd notice when I do things right."

Needless to say, I was shaken. I had never meant to give my son the message that he had to be like me. However, he was right that I had expectations of him and wanted him to change in certain ways. He was letting me know that he was not thrilled with everything about my plan for him. He let me know that his hairstyle would probably never match mine, his clothing choices would not be the same as mine, his choice of friends would not always pass muster in my book. He was giving me due warning that he was not always going to meet my expectations of him. Fair enough.

Many of our behaviors are designed to control and manipulate others into changing into something that is more suitable to our temperament. Sometimes those expectations are realistic, but sometimes they are not. In almost all instances, however, our expectations for someone else will be met by resistance. Talking openly about that resistance can help us avoid power struggles. Power struggles do not work. Both people lose in the long run.

I cannot say my son and I had smooth sailing from that point on. We occasionally engaged in power struggles, and sometimes felt very frustrated. But I was usually able to choose my battles, let minor issues remain minor, and give him choices on the major ones.

You don't have to be a counselor to recognize that few people really want to change. Even when in distress, most of us look for easy ways around issues so that we won't have to make significant adjustments. If we have a stress headache, most of us are inclined to take an aspirin rather than make deep, cumbersome lifestyle changes. When we are at odds with our partner, we are most likely to blame him or her for the problem rather than look at our part in the fray. We want easy solutions and will resist the rigors of true personality change. Greg and Patricia both wanted an easy solution to a dicey problem. They must face the fact that an easy answer is not forthcoming. They may be in for a very long haul.

Resistance to change often takes the form of *regression*. We want to live in the past holding on to old communication habits. We do not want to plow ahead through rocky soil. Scott Peck, in *Further Along the Road Less Traveled*, reminds us that when we were banished from Eden, we were banished forever. He tells us that we must grow up and become increasingly conscious of the conditions of our life. This is painful, he asserts, and many choose to numb themselves so that they do not have to feel the pain. But to grow up, to face life's challenges, means to let go of the crutches we all use to avoid life, and to face the real issues. As Peck said in the opening line of *The Road Less Traveled*, "Life is difficult." Indeed it is.

As you reflect on these issues, you may want to consider how you and your partner avoid facing the tough problems in your relationship. What are the difficulties you try to avoid, and how do you try to avoid them?

As we watch Patricia and Greg struggle in their dance with the spending issue, we can see that neither want it to destroy their wonderful new love life. We can relate. Many of our relationships have issues that appear inconsequential but will linger as corrosive elements until we solve them.

Tactics to Avoid Change

This book addresses many of the tactics we use to avoid change, so I will simply offer some of the more obvious diversions here. Many more will be discussed in other chapters, but for now, consider this list:

- blaming our partner for our problems
- talking around issues and being evasive
- being playful to avoid the seriousness of the moment
- retreating into silence and pouting
- being "busy" to avoid talking or working through problems
- offering simplistic, unrealistic solutions that can't last
- being deceptive

What might these avoidance tactics sound like in a conversation? Let me offer some examples:

> Denial: "I don't need to change. This isn't really a problem."

> Blaming: "You're the one making a big deal out of things. It's your problem."

> Avoidance: "Leave me alone. I don't want to talk about it."

Minimization: "Sure, it's a problem, but what's the big deal? You're making mountains out of molehills. It's not like I'm gambling our savings away."

Playfulness: "Come here and give me a hug. Let's not allow this problem to come between us."

Oversimplification: "No sweat. I've quit smoking before, and I can do it again. It won't be a problem."

Pouting: "You're always picking on me. I can never seem to do enough to please you."

Do you see yourself or your partner in any of those responses? Can you think of other tactics you or your partner have used to avoid facing serious issues?

One of my favorite authors, Rainer Maria Rilke, talks at length about the complexities of love and relationship. He reminds us of the sobriety of love in his work *Rilke on Love and Other Difficulties:*

Like so much else, people have also misunderstood the place of love in life, they have made it into play and pleasure because they thought that play and pleasure were more blissful than work; but there is nothing happier than work, and love, just because it is the extreme happiness, can be nothing else but work. So, whoever loves must try to act as if he had a great work.[1]

What Does Change Require of Us?

If change does not just happen and most of us resist it with a wide variety of tactics, how can we reach our lofty goals? What must we do to change?

In my book *See Dick and Jane Grow Up* I list several steps required for true change to occur.

Own your own stuff. You must take responsibility for the circumstances in your life and what you have done to get where you are today. After all, you are not where you are by accident. You have played an active role in getting exactly where you are. At the same time, you must not take responsibility for anyone else. For example, Greg chose to start spending excessively, not Patricia. He must take ownership of that problem. You are not responsible for your partner's irresponsible behavior. You cannot change someone else. But you can change you, and that is where you need to begin.

Put on the cloak of courageous humility. This means you must take off the rose-colored glasses and be prepared to see things as they are. This takes far more courage than we might think. Few are ready to see things as they are, but this can lead to significant change.

Steven, a middle-aged man, came to my office wanting more affection from his wife. He was very frustrated and hid behind a veneer of righteousness. He recounted to me all the ways that he was living a bold, Christian life: He sang in the choir, taught Sunday school classes, and belonged to a men's prayer group. Yet in spite of his impressive résumé, he could not get his wife to warm to him. He was baffled.

We spent a number of weeks exploring his frustrations. Indeed, we struggled to find anything that he had done wrong, and I was prepared to offer him the platitude that he was not responsible for her behavior, only his own. I assumed that she was experiencing something that would give way to more demonstrative behavior in time. However, I asked her to come in so that I could get the full story.

She was more than willing to share her side of the story, and it differed from his significantly. From her perspective, Steven was a very demanding man. He criticized her at every turn. She was even afraid of offering an opinion that differed from his. She believed that the only part of her that she could retain was her affection. She felt guilty doing so, but she simply could no longer allow herself to feel helpless. She had tried to tell him about her frustrations, but he responded with religious homilies. He offered her regular advice on how to choose her friends, what kinds of clothing to buy, and how to be more frugal with their money.

When I shared with Steven what I had learned from his wife, he was a bit shaken, but he nodded his understanding. Her observations had not fallen on deaf ears. He had held on to his controlling nature as long as possible. The time had come to make changes, and he seemed open to the possibility. He showed that he was willing to "put on the cloak of humility," though doing so was difficult for him.

Fight the familiar misery. All of us have wasted time languishing in the same old ruts. As the saying goes, many of us are not only stuck in a rut but have decorated it as well.

Fighting the familiar misery is a rigorous process that we should not minimize. In fact, one of the primary reasons people do not obtain lasting change is that they fail to count the costs. Change is very difficult, and one must never assume that it will be easy, quick, or permanent. Greg, for example, has cut back on his spending before but doesn't seem willing to fight the issue on a permanent basis.

Get help. We cannot change alone. As I mentioned previously, we can only change ourselves, but having people behind us certainly helps. Not only do we need our own personal cheering section, such as a support group, supportive friends, or a spouse, but we also need the transforming power of God. As the psalmist understood, God desires "truth in the inner parts" (Psalm 51:6). Alcoholics Anonymous calls it "rigorous honesty."

There Was a Little Man

Perhaps you recall the story of Nicodemus as told by the apostle John (John 3). It is an interesting story concerning the issue of change. The story opens with Nicodemus as a high-ranking member of the Jewish council and therefore in an adversarial position with Jesus and His teachings. Yet in spite of his vast knowledge and extensive education, he realizes that he still needs to learn some things. He feels that emptiness in his gut that Blaise Pascal has aptly described as a God-shaped vacuum that God alone can fill. Nicodemus knows that his life is not working and that he needs change.

He comes to Jesus at night, presumably so that no one would know. He questions Jesus about His strange teachings and miraculous signs.

Jesus tells Nicodemus what many of us have come to experience. Jesus says, "No one can see the kingdom of God unless he is born again" (John 3:3). Jesus is describing a revolutionary change, not simply a cosmetic one. It is a complete turn from old ways, a conversion. Without this, only superficial changes will result, and a little change is not nearly enough. The old habits, troubles, and complications of life return in full vigor, sometimes tenfold. But true conversion can bring real transformation and lasting satisfaction.

What did Nicodemus do with this outrageous advice? Did he experience conversion? Was he born again? The new birth may have sounded bizarre and impossible, but something must have changed inside him, for he later brought a mixture of myrrh and aloes for Jesus' burial. His covert visit early in Jesus' public ministry led to an open display of affection, admiration, and loyalty at its end.

One must surmise that Nicodemus had to count the cost of his newfound loyalty to Christ. His Jewish colleagues could not have been happy with his new disposition and allegiance. His status undoubtedly changed, but his conversion was worth the price. He had counted the cost of change and decided he had more to gain by changing than he had to lose. This is a truth that each of us must weigh for ourselves as well. When we change, we will lose some things from our old life. But we will gain so much more.

An Honest Appraisal

When Patricia was truly honest with herself, she realized that the spending issue ran deeper than she wanted to admit. His credit card debt and constant desire for more and more toys represented a habit that was destined to strain their relationship. She was fully aware that not everyone felt as she did. She knew many friends lived for today and, like Greg, had repeatedly maxed out their credit cards. But for her, this was not an option, and most importantly, she expected to be able to talk about Greg's spending without running up against his excessive defensiveness. She reflected on the image of the stinky elephant and decided she no longer wished to dodge the smelly mess.

As she delved more deeply into her feelings, she realized that Greg's spending and his inability to talk about it with her affected her view of him. She lost respect for him and felt embarrassed by his immature behavior. His inability to control his spending was a sign of weakness. She did not want to live this way, to compromise her financial integrity. The more honest she became with herself, the more prepared she was for an honest encounter with Greg. Things needed to change, and she was beginning to realize what that change would demand of her and of him. This realization made her options clearer to her. The clarity she gained gave her peace, and she had a sense of purpose that she wanted to convey to Greg. They had their talk one evening after work.

"Greg, I want to talk to you about your spending. I know this is a touchy topic, but we need to discuss it. Can we do that?"

"Sure, but I don't know what there is to talk about."

"I don't like the fact that you have two credit cards charged to the limit, and yet you still want to buy more gadgets for your stereo. I'm not comfortable with that kind of spending and want to be in a partnership where we learn how to save and spend appropriately."

"I always make my credit card payments and have never been late. Why are you saying that I overspend?"

"But Greg, you are paying 18 percent interest on those cards. I'm not comfortable with that."

"Patricia, that's your problem. You're not comfortable with it. I am. It's my money, and until we are married you shouldn't be worried about the way I spend my money. Can't you see that?"

"I disagree. We are thinking about getting married and are beginning to blend our lives together. Your spending is becoming my concern, and I think you should begin to have some say about how I manage my life too. We have to start making compromises with one another."

"I'm not willing to have you tell me how to spend my money, Patricia. I work very hard every day and like to buy nice things for myself. I deserve them, and I don't think it's fair for you to try to control me. You control your money, I'll control mine."

"But you don't control your money. That's the problem. It's controlling you. And I don't think you're hearing a word I'm saying about how I feel, knowing that you are a slave to your credit cards. I feel less important than your toys."

Both sat looking at one another for a moment. Greg turned away, sighing heavily. Patricia looked down and began to cry.

"The bottom line is that it's my problem, Patricia, and I'll deal with it in my time, in my way."

"Greg, I don't like to see you do something that I know will really harm you in the long run. I lose respect for you when I see you act responsibly in every other area of your life and then lose it when it comes to toys. You seem to be a compulsive spender, and I wonder if spending will end up being a major issue in our relationship. I wonder if you'll be able to handle it if we have a mortgage and children. We can't seem to talk about it now. How will we talk about it later?"

What Makes Him Tick?

In spite of his partner's obvious distress, naggings, and pleas, Greg continues to spend. Why? What is happening inside Greg during this ordeal? My guess is that Greg is experiencing a mixture of feelings.

He probably feels misunderstood. He is being genuine when he says he does not feel badly about his spending. He has been this way for years and has never had to be accountable to another person since living with his parents. He does not understand Patricia's difficulty living with his irresponsible spending.

He feels resentment. He wants not only to spend the way he wants but also for her to quit nagging him. He enjoys his lifestyle and is attached to it. Changes would be difficult for him to make. He has already run that scenario over in his mind and knows that change would be very hard for him. He knows how accustomed he has become to spending his paycheck on toys for himself. Having to take her opinion into account on a regular basis is a threat to him.

He feels fear. He can sense that part of his personal identity may be coming to an end. Is this what marriage is like? How much will he have to give up in order to be in relationship with Patricia? Questions flood his mind, issues that had never been issues before. He realizes that their relationship is in jeopardy. As with any of us facing change, he wonders what the results will be if he is unable or unwilling to change.

He feels concerned about being controlled in the future. He wonders if he will constantly have to change to meet her expectations.

He feels a curious sense of relief. The issue is clearly and bluntly out on the table. They are really beginning to talk to one another. Not without significant defensiveness, but they are talking. With the veil of deceit ripped away, he and Patricia now stand face-to-face with the problem.

Now What?

Now that Patricia and Greg have had their discussion and stared into the eye of the problem, what are they to do?

Is their world now smaller or larger than ever before? I suggest that it is larger and filled with more hope than ever. They face new challenges, but now they can measure the cost and take appropriate steps toward a successful outcome. They are now in a position to make a new agreement about Greg's spending. What course of action is he willing to commit to? How will they measure his success? What will Patricia's role be in the change process? What kind of support is she willing to offer? These are aspects of a healthy agreement that can bring them closer together as a team working on this problem.

Perhaps your situation is similar in some way to Patricia and Greg's. I suspect that you can find some of your story in theirs. All of us, at one time or another, have been stumped when determining how to make lasting changes in our relationships.

Regardless of what you tell yourself or what your partner has told you, change is difficult. But it is possible if you agree to be honest with yourself, count the cost, and proceed with deliberation and faith.

Six

It Can Be So Much Better

Then I asked: Does a firm persuasion that a thing is so,
make it so? He replied: All poets believe that it does,
and in ages of imagination this firm persuasion
removed mountains; but many are not capable
of a firm persuasion of anything.

WILLIAM BLAKE

Recently, I was sitting at my desk listening to Kenny G perform his magic on "Somewhere Over the Rainbow." I could visualize Judy Garland belting out the words that have carried millions away to another land. Why has that song made generations of folks swoon? Certainly Kenny G has incredible lyrical talent that makes us melt into the music. But the real magic is in the words, which tease us with the possibility that true love will someday find us. That skies of blue are the backdrop for our future, and dreams that we dare to dream really do come true.

We relate to romantic dreams in two distinct ways. Some say that romance is the domain of 16-year-olds, a realm where lust and infatuation run amok. After the initial flare of passion subsides, some couples contend that romance belonged to their youth. They are adults now, and the time has come to get down to the business of raising a family, paying the bills, and planning for retirement.

Others believe that romance will always have its place. They still watch *Sleepless in Seattle,* sigh deeply, and dream of injecting a little bit of that chemistry back into their relationship. What would meeting our soul mate on Valentine's Day on top of the Empire State Building feel like? As we watch the movie, we know Tom Hanks and Meg Ryan will find each other and live happily ever after. That's the way things turn out in feel-good "chick flicks." *They must find one another,* we think. And happily, they do. Once again we are convinced that love prevails.

My hunch is that both groups are partly right. Reality pulls all of us back to a pragmatic world. Bills must be paid. The kids need to be taken to the dentist. The house needs to be cleaned before company arrives on Saturday. But we can't quite silence the young girl or boy inside us who wants to be loved, cherished, even adored. Would someone really travel across the continent to find us? After we have found someone who cares for us, can we hang on to the wonderful feelings? That is the stuff of our dreams, and these desires are integral parts of the way we have been created: to dream, to hope, to seek.

And here is our fifth secret for a wonderful relationship: You must believe that you don't have to settle for something mediocre. *Your relationship really can be so much better than it is.* Mediocrity is not what God had in mind when he created woman and man, relationships, and marriage.

We read in the story of creation that God made man in His own the image. He created man to be relational. This certainly seems to resonate with our desire to be in a healthy, committed, caring relationship. God decided that for the man to be alone was not good. So He created woman. Imagine Adam's mouth gaping open as he tried to utter something intelligible when he first set his eyes on Eve: "This is now bone of my bones and flesh of my flesh; she shall be called 'woman,' for she was taken out of man" (Genesis 2:23). God had high aspirations for how two people could come together, helping each other to be more complete and satisfied than either could possibly be alone. Yes, our relationships can be so much better than they are.

> He has made everything beautiful in its time. He has also set eternity in the hearts of men (Ecclesiastes 3:11).

Johannes Brahms' Lullaby

Another fabulous Kenny G tune is his rendition of "Brahms' Lullaby." Kenny G is able to inject something mysterious into our hearts with this bedtime song by Brahms. The words of this classic speak of a mother's adoration for her child, and they stir a lingering hope that we can gain that kind of affection from another person. Is it possible?

The other evening I had a conversation with a woman who took time in the middle of our phone call to get her son ready for bed. At first, I was slightly annoyed. I felt as if I were eavesdropping on her family life while I waited. But then I stopped thinking about myself and listened to her gentleness with him. I heard him ask for a bear hug before heading off to sleep. I couldn't see them, but I know she embraced him. I heard her tell him how much she loved him. She spoke words of encouragement to him and told him how special he was to her. I have no doubt that he went to sleep peacefully. "Brahms' Lullaby" in action.

Could all of us still be looking for that sense of being special? Could we still want someone special to find us irresistible? I think so. I don't think that longing ever disappears. It may get obscured by laundry lists, bills, and dirty diapers, but it never disappears.

I had the privilege of being close to my two sons during their infancy. Neither would rest until they had their good-night kiss and goodnight hug. My youngest, especially, resisted sleep until I complied with his nightly ritual. Even when I worked late into the evening, he would awaken to ask for his special touch. I needed it just as much as he did. This ritual lasted longer than either of us will publicly admit. As my sons grew older, I wondered if such rituals were still necessary, but I quickly decided they could do no harm. In fact, they seemed to bind us together in invisible ways. We still kiss and hug to this day, without embarrassment, as they grow into young men. Until they tell me to stop, I will shower them with love and affection every time we meet.

Dan and Debra

From my professional viewpoint, Dan and Debra are an unusual couple. They came to see me much later in their marital life than the typical couple. They are 60 and 62 years old, respectively. Both are accomplished professionals and are nearing retirement. Unfortunately, the hopes they had for their relationship have never materialized.

Dan and Debra have both worked hard all of their lives. Probably considered to be type A personalities, they are degreed, certified, and have résumés as long as my arm. They have three wonderful grown children with whom they have excellent relationships. With four adorable grandchildren, they have much to be thankful for. Their professional careers are winding down, and they now find themselves talking to financial planners about how to maintain their current lifestyle. To the outside observer, they are living the American dream: robust professional careers, a long list of notable accomplishments, delightful children and grandchildren, and time and money to enjoy them and their other interests.

They have enjoyed far more than the external trappings of success. As I came to know and observe them in the "clinical hour," I realized they genuinely like one another. They exchange glances as though comforting one another when they talk about tough issues. They share laughter at one another's foibles. She teases him about being a romance novel junkie. He jokes about her being comfortable under the hood of a car.

But this apparently happy story has a significant caveat. It appears just below the surface, beyond the view of their children and friends and often beyond the scope of their daily conversations. Dan has had several indiscretions during their 40-year marriage, one fairly recently. Debra tries to conceal her pain, but she winces as more of the truth is revealed. The distance between them becomes more apparent each time they are candid with one another. They came to see, slowly, that they have had an intimacy issue for years.

They sought help because they want more from the relationship. They share a sense of urgency. As if in a belated mid-life crisis, both are making final evaluations as to whether they can sustain their relationship into their twilight years.

Counseling with Dan and Debra is at once delightfully humorous and poignantly painful. The closer I get to the real picture, the more I see how alienated they are. They have covered over years of hurt and pain with other experiences. But time has been inadequate to soothe their wounded hearts.

As I work with them, I cannot help but wonder how many other couples have wounds that reopen periodically, without receiving a doctor's attention. Are Dan and Debra unique, I wonder, or do they represent a vast number of folks that strongly desire more of the romance that they had in their earlier years? Why has Dan sought affection outside the relationship, and what has been the lasting impact on Debra and their marriage?

During one of our first sessions, I asked each of them to talk a bit about the other and about their relationship. "Dan has always been a hard-working, loving man," Debra said. "In the early years he spent a lot of time away from home, working as a sales representative. He was made to sell, and he is good at it. He has been very successful, and I am very proud of him. He has provided for our family beyond my expectations. But I have never really felt like I had all of his heart. Whenever I get close, I feel him push me away. I think he is afraid of intimacy. He won't share his feelings with me, and he seems to be afraid to lean on me, even after all our years together. For some reason, he is capable of being emotionally attached with other women but not with me. I just passed his detachment off as something to do with his upbringing and hoped it would get better with time.

"He is a strong Christian. I admire his commitment to his faith. He is a principled man, generally a man of integrity. He would never cheat anyone and often puts others' interests ahead of his own. I sometimes think he lets people take advantage of him. I love Dan; I like being with him. But I know that he's not totally committed to me."

"Debra is the joy of my life," Dan said. "I admire her professional abilities so much. She is the best computer analyst in the business. She can do things with that box that I think would be impossible for most techs. She is truly amazing.

"Debra is my best friend. She is willing to do anything for me, and I care about her deeply. That's why I can't explain why I've had the affairs. It just seems to be a weakness in my personality. I'm always looking over the fence at the greener grass. I don't do it to hurt her or because of anything she is doing wrong. It's my problem. There always seems to be something in the way of us coming together in an intimate way. I wonder if we have been too busy to really connect with each other. Sometimes I think I just feel bored with the whole thing."

I asked Dan and Debra what they had done to try to correct the problem. I was surprised by their answers. Both had basically agreed to pretend that the problem did not exist. Both had assumed that "these kinds of things happen in the best of marriages" and were mostly content to enjoy the strengths of their relationship and ignore the weaknesses. Both had resigned themselves to a "good relationship" and had never seriously considered pursuing an excellent, vibrant relationship, free from distractions. Neither had ever held a better relationship clearly in view or considered it a possibility. Their focus, it seemed, had been on building a home, family, and hefty retirement account—to the exclusion of their relationship.

"I just assumed that what we had was good enough," Debra said. "I have been through my share of pain, but when I listen to my friends, I don't think I have it any worse than they do. After all, Dan and I are still together after 40 years of marriage."

A Limited Vision

The most serious problem facing Dan and Debra is one of vision. Or rather, a lack of it. How could each have settled for what they have for so long? They suffer from what the poet Blake described as a lack of "firm persuasion." They do not have an inner conviction that their love life can be anything other than what it is at the moment. But it can be so much more. Somewhere, perhaps deep in their hearts, I suspect they know that this is true.

Many people seem to approach marriage with a fatalistic point of view. Filled with a dull sense of ennui, they look around and see few examples of anything better. They see other couples blindly heading down the path that leads to growing apathy, but they have little hope that anything can be better. Where are the guides who would encourage us to risk everything for passionate love? Are the tender words and bold vision only for the poets? Most people seem to think so.

David Whyte, author of the splendid work *Crossing the Unknown Sea*, talks about passion in a way that should be applied to marriage:

Life is a creative, intimate and unpredictable conversation if it is nothing else, spoken or unspoken, and our life and our work are both the result of the particular way we hold that passionate conversation. In Blake's sense, a firm persuasion was a form of self-knowledge; it was understood as a result, an outcome, a bounty that came from paying close attention to an astonishing world and the way each of us is made differently and uniquely for that world.[1]

Let's look closely at this quote again and pick out the applicable principles for our work here. We need...

- creativity, intimacy, unpredictability
- passion
- self-knowledge
- close attention to the astonishing world
- conviction that each of us is made differently for our world

Consider for a moment the extent to which you are living in creative, intimate, unpredictable, and passionate conversation. Life is predictable in many ways, lacking spontaneity and zest. At times, we all wish that our paths included zigs and zags to keep things fresh. We all want to avoid the boredom that can stagnate the best of relationships.

Shadowbound

A man once lived as a prisoner in the desert. He was a prisoner because he had developed the habit of following his shadow. It was a relentless and unbending compass that he obeyed completely and followed without question. Every morning when the sun came up he began walking in the direction his shadow pointed. Obviously, following this course day in and day out meant that he made little progress in his life. He never traveled far enough to leave the desert, but his path was familiar and comfortable.

He often wondered what facing the sun would be like instead of always turning his back to it and walking the other way. One morning a voice came to him saying, *Just stop it. Could the change be that simple?* he wondered. What a lovely thought. But along with hope and anticipation, the new voice also brought fear and dread.

The next time the sun came up, he felt the powerful tug of his shadow. He was unable to resist it. But finally, one day he summoned the strength and vision to turn in a new direction. He was astonished—the rising sun in front of him was brighter and more wonderful than he had imagined anything could ever be. Each day the pull of his shadow decreased. Slowly, he put one foot in front of the other, uncertain of where he was going but sure that he at least was not going in circles in the desert. And he did not feel alone anymore.[2]

While Dan and Debra have sustained a relationship for 40 years, one cannot help but wonder whether they have been following their shadows in the desert. Are they so bound to old ways of doing things that they cannot see beyond the sandy dunes of their parched relationship? How many other couples are eking out an existence from barren land? Are they aware that an oasis is just beyond their view?

> *Thirsty hearts are those whose longings have been wakened by the touch of God within them.*
>
> —A.W. Tozer

The Promised Land

The scouting report was dismal. The Israelites desperately needed rest after wandering in the wilderness for 40 years. But the prospects did not look good. The spies reported seeing giants and warned that the land devoured those living in it. *Great,* they must have thought. *This is the land filled with milk and honey, promised to a weary people?*

But their leader, Joshua, determined that what God had promised them must surely be true, sent out his own scouts for a second opinion. He wanted more; he needed another perspective. God would not have made the promises if they were not true.

So Joshua sent a second band of spies into the land to check out the situation. Sure enough, the second report was much more favorable. "The LORD has surely given the whole land into our hands; all the people are melting in fear because of us" (Joshua 2:24). The biblical account of Joshua leading the Israelites into the promised land is a wonderful illustration of God fulfilling His promise to His people after they have demonstrated their obedience. It is an illustration to us that what we see at first glance may not be all that is available to us. Much more awaits us if we will believe and follow His leadership.

What Is Possible?

After hearing the story of Joshua, we can proclaim loudly to Dan and Debra, "Don't settle, folks. Don't meander around in the desert when rivers of living water are available to all who seek them." But is that the spiritual message beneath the metaphor of desert living? What does God say is available for marriages? What is the vision that we can seek?

Larry Crabb, in his classic book *The Marriage Builder,* shares God's intentions about marriage:

> God created us in His image, personal beings unlike all other creatures, and like Him in our unique capacity for relationship. As dependent personal beings, we cannot function fully according to our design without close relationships. I understand the Scriptures to teach that relationships offer two

elements that are absolutely essential if we are to live as God intended: (1) the security of being truly loved and accepted, and (2) the significance of making a substantial, lasting, positive impact on another person.[3]

There it is. Our vision for a relationship that we can rest upon. God has provided a way for us to find security and significance. We can find the security of knowing that we are loved and accepted for who we are. Certainly we each need some refining. We are all in process. But we need to be in a relationship where we are secure. This most certainly was not the case for Dan and Debra. She could not feel secure with Dan wandering outside the boundaries of their marriage. And Dan also needs to feel secure and content within the bounds of marriage. This is his ultimate desire.

The relationship must also be significant. We need to be certain that we are having an impact on another human being. We can see this is missing with Dan and Debra. They don't feel as though they are impacting each another in a significant way. They have elected to find meaning and value outside of their marriage, primarily through their work and their relationships with friends and family. Their marriage has suffered as a result.

What is the vision for a successful marriage?

- Marriage is a safe environment in which we can be completely open, be vulnerable, heal, and grow.
- Marriage is a relationship in which we can experiment with different aspects of our nature, being playful, creative, spiritual, honest, intellectual, and adventurous.
- Marriage includes joyful, romantic love and physical, emotional, and spiritual union.
- Marriage is a refuge from the stresses and struggles of everyday life.

- Marriage is an opportunity to come home to be with our best friend in loving companionship.

Does this sound impossible for you? If so, I hope that you will dream with me about the day when these possibilities will become your reality. They are possibilities, but only if both people share the vision.

What Makes Him Tick?

Let's try to understand what Dan might be thinking. Why couldn't a man who has had the world at the tips of his fingers create and sustain intimacy with his wife of 40 years?

Dan is typical in many ways. He has sought to "conquer and destroy" the business world as he was taught to do. He focused his energies on being the best sales representative in his field. He wanted to be a financial success and has been. However, while he was busy providing all the extra niceties for his family, they were drifting out of his circle of true intimacy. He has not focused on creating warmth, sustenance, and safety for his wife. He rarely asked her what she needs from him. His wild heart was depleted in the workplace, and nothing was left for his marriage.

Lest we heap all of the responsibility on Dan, we must remember that Debra has also been a focused woman. She concentrated on raising their three children and developing her own professional career. She bought into the "golden handcuffs" and lost sight of their vision for intimacy.

But Dan bears the larger portion of blame. He was raised by a man much like himself. His father worked through the Depression years, and making a living was tantamount to being a man. Society expected the wife to stand by, understanding that "a man needed to do what a man needed to do." She was supposed to be understanding and patient and accepting of the leftovers she would receive. But that philosophy does not fare well. It was the mold out of which Dan came, but it was poor advice.

To Dan's credit, he was willing to change. Gradually, over the course of several months, he reoriented his thinking to making his marriage work. He applied one of his tried-and-true business principles to his marriage: You can always make something work more effectively. The change has been difficult, but to make his marriage work, Dan has learned a new set of rules:

- Relationships require as much work and focus as any business.
- Love and affection are not superfluous but necessary ingredients of a good marriage.
- Learning the fine art of conversation is critical to building and maintaining a good relationship.
- His wife deserves for him to be loyal to her, to honor her, and to cherish her.
- A safe environment requires commitment.

Now What?

Dan and Debra have been coming to counseling for several months and are committed to correcting years of problems, so they are learning new skills. Dan is trying to pass Relationship Building 101. He actually likes to learn and is willing to try new things. Debra is pleased with the results. They appear to be headed for a stronger, better relationship than ever.

However, the growth is not without work on Debra's part too. In fact, perhaps the lion's share of the work has been hers. She has had to critically look at all the ways that she has settled for so little in their marriage. She has had to realize that she became "small" in their relationship so that he could be "big." Their marriage was all about him, and she settled for that kind of mentality. She assumed that was the way marriage had to be and slipped into her small role naturally. In order to grow, she has had to examine all the ways she conceded to him, failed to share her opinion, or fussed and fumed but did little else to set a valid boundary. She had to understand why she ignored or denied the magnitude of his philandering. She came to realize that she was devaluing their marriage by minimizing his adultery. She has had to work on deep-seated self-esteem issues.

Now that both are taking responsibility for their parts in the marriage, they have reason for optimism. They have a clearer vision and hope for things to be much better. Already they are seeing the rewards that come from acknowledging a problem, looking at the causes for it, and agreeing upon a solution. They are really talking with one another, sometimes painfully, and are sharing a new level of intimacy. Now they have the hope that they can enjoy another 40 years together—or at least 25!

Seven

A Little Change Is Not Enough

Never look down to test the ground before
taking your next step: only he who keeps his
eye fixed on the far horizon will find his right road.

DAG HAMMARSKJØLD

I watched with more than a little angst as she slipped out of the harbor under obvious duress. The waves were large, the winter winds brisk. She was a low-slung, sleek little sloop of hand-tooled mahogany. She heeled over in the face of winds that blasted into the cove from the north. I watched as the gusts filled her sails, seemingly catching the skipper off guard. He was in danger of an accidental jibe, and he hadn't yet left the harbor.

Why is he taking her out today? I wondered. Surely he could find far better conditions for practicing the craft of sailing. Even worse, from the looks of things, he was a novice. I watched him tack back and forth in a haphazard fashion, wondering how long he would last before crumpling his boat against a piling. Despite the conditions and his ineptness, he was intent upon getting out of the harbor into bigger water.

I watched him with concern and humor. The situation was certainly of his own making. A wiser beginner would have taken lessons from a real pro, but apparently he preferred to learn by himself in spite of the risks. A rapid swing of the tiller here and an overcorrection there left him flailing about like a piece of driftwood pitched to and fro by the incoming tide. What was his destination? Did he know how to navigate these waters? Did he even have a destination in mind?

I imagined that this initiate to the sailing club would one day learn how to sail. But would he master the art, or would he be content to meander about on his small vessel, doing just enough to stay afloat?

Novice sailors are not the only ones buffeted by winds of gale force. I am told that even in this age of computer technology, jet airliners are off course most of the time. Due to traffic congestion, wind, rain, turbulence, and other elements, planes have to make constant corrections to arrive safely at their destinations. And because they rely on good advice and sound calculations, they most often arrive without incident.

We are much like the skipper of the sailboat. We need to regularly compare the direction of our lives with our desired goals. We can often make small corrections that get us headed in the right direction. But sometimes, small corrections are not enough. Sometimes we get far off course and need to make major adjustments. Unfortunately, we rarely take our emotional compass and map in hand and chart significant changes in our life's direction, even if radical change is necessary. And that brings us to our sixth secret: For real change to occur, for us to get all that we can out of life, *a little change is not enough.*

John and Jillian

John and Jillian have learned to be satisfied with little bits of change. Married for 13 years, they had been relatively happy for most of them. When they were unhappy, they were able to talk about their problems with a candor that many couples don't enjoy. But they had several problems that kept surfacing. They decided they would simply try to weather the storm and hope for better days. They had not been utterly truthful with themselves about the depths of their problems and certainly had not been willing to commit to making significant change. They had tried for years to tweak their relationship, hoping that would solve their problems. But after 13 years, they were finally ready to admit that a little change is often not enough.

Both John and Jillian brought baggage to their marriage, as most people do. John was a nice enough man and a devout Christian. Yet he had a secret life that included occasional marijuana use. In his earlier days he had used quite heavily and even sold it for a while. Over the years he had seen the effects the drug had on his personality, such as a lack of motivation and some symptoms of depression. Under strong pressure from Jillian, he cut back to using only every few weeks. He always used discreetly so that their children would not suspect anything. As time went on, however, his secret habit did not disappear as Jillian had hoped it would, and she increasingly feared that their children would discover it. After years of coaching their children about the ill effects of drugs, she did not want to give them a flagrantly mixed message.

Jillian had been tolerant of John's habit for years. She even smoked pot with him during their college days. She accepted it as part of their social life. But as time went by and their girls got older, she found herself increasingly embarrassed by John's use. She felt convicted that this habit was not consistent with their values or religious beliefs.

Their attempts to solve the problem had all failed. Jillian would confront John about his marijuana use, and he would become remorseful and talk about quitting completely. He would offer her extra gifts and affection, and this would lull her into a sense of complacency. John could be a very charming man when he wanted to be. He knew how to make Jillian happy. Flowers, affection, warmth, and caring came quite naturally to him. He truly loved her and wanted things to work out for them. At times, however, he could not see how smoking a little marijuana once a month could hurt anything. But in his more critical moments, he reluctantly admitted that marijuana could not continue to be a part of his life as a Christian husband and father.

Jillian did not want something like this to destroy her marriage. She enjoyed her life with John and admired him greatly. He worked as a fifth grade teacher and had a wonderful reputation. He also coached the high school basketball team. Gregarious and fun-loving, he was an easy man to care about. They had so much going for them; she was annoyed that they had to struggle constantly with his repulsive habit. She feared others in the church would find out about it and wondered if there were other spouses with the same dilemma.

Cycles of Confrontation

Couples often repeat patterns of confrontation in their marriages. When Jillian and John came for counseling, we were able to identify and monitor some of their patterns. They seemed to mimic the cycles of destructive conflict that occur in the relationships of many of my clients.

The *tension-building* phase comes first. In this stage, one or both partners may notice that things are not quite right. Perhaps one notices the problem but tries to ignore it. They may navigate around the problem, but this does nothing to reduce the anxiety they are feeling. Neither may come straight out and talk about it, but sooner or later both realize that they are becoming increasingly irritable around each other.

Bickering may occur about other incidental issues. Fighting may break out over someone leaving a towel on the bathroom floor or dishes in the sink. A pall is cast over the home, though neither identifies it as such.

Finally the tension becomes too great for the couple to handle, and it leads to the second phase: *explosion*. Their marriage has become a tinderbox ready for ignition. There are too many incendiary devises lying around, just waiting to be used. Sooner or later, the husband and wife let go of the inhibitions that have been keeping them mute, and the fight is on. Sometimes it is over the real issue, as in Jillian and John's case, but it may also be about something utterly ridiculous. Sometimes the couple has the insight to see the real issue and deal with it. More often, however, the fight becomes personal and fails to account for the underlying problem. Consequently, nothing gets settled.

The fire may burn for a few minutes, or it may rage for days. Couples who do not know how to disagree effectively may spew and sputter at one another for hours, leaving them exhausted without ever dealing with the real issue. Having emotionally drained themselves, the couple is often ready to make up. This phase, *remorse and contrition*, may include sincere apologies and promises to change. He may offer flowers and assurances to seek help. These assurances are typically shallow, short-lived, and meaningless. As we have discussed previously, unless real action is taken, real change will not occur. Couples in situations like the one I described rarely undertake real change. But his flowers and affection go a long way to temporarily assuaging her anger and frustration. In fact, in this phase both get the sense that the problems can be managed and they can still enjoy the many wonderful qualities of their relationship.

Researchers have studied this pattern at length. Many believe that the cycle itself is somewhat addicting. Tension building, explosion, and making up. Can you relate to these patterns?

Theorists have suggested a few explanations for the intractable nature of this routine. The cycle of tension building, explosions, and remorse, replicated many times over the years, becomes a sort of super-glue, binding one partner to another. Rather than alienating them, it does just the opposite. It has been called *trauma bonding*, and if you believe that to be too severe of a name, think again.

Trauma bonding can be a useful term in explaining very destructive relationships, but I believe it can also be used to sort out what happens in "normal" marriages every day. The couple has an issue they cannot seem to resolve, they bicker about it and eventually have some kind of explosion, followed by a romantic interlude that cements the pattern in place. As the central characters in the movie *The Story of Us* so poignantly say, "For better or worse, this is the story of us. It is our story."

And so it goes. A little change here, a little change there, falling back into old patterns, and true change never occurs. Old routines are comfortable, and rocking the boat is nobody's idea of fun. If you desire real change, be prepared to endure a bout of seasickness.

The False Trajectory

Like the inexperienced sailboat skipper, many people drift through life, making little progress toward their destination. Lacking a clearly defined goal and a well-marked course of action, they meander around, making one small turn after another. In fact, many do not fully understand what progress would look like because they are so busy navigating daily challenges. They fail to set a long-term trajectory that establishes where they want to go. When they discover that their relationship is heading in the wrong direction, a small correction often fails to get them back on course.

Sailors have a term, *the waypoint*, for marking progress toward a charted destination. Good sailors always know where they are and where their goal is. They do not want to be caught unawares, for the cost could be tragic. The same is true of marriages.

I remember meeting Sarah, a sharp and beautiful woman who was quite unhappy in her marriage. She wanted to be happy and hoped that I had a magic pill that would quickly salve her open wound.

From the opening moments of our meeting I could see that she was not only unhappy and impatient but very angry as well. Bitterness oozed from her, and I felt uneasy in her presence. Sarah, on the other hand, seemed to be strangely at home with her resentment. She had walked closely with it for many years, though something was causing her to question it now.

She probably would still be living with her anger but for the recent loss of a close friend. Two years earlier she had lost a parent to an untimely death, and now, in the middle of a vibrant and active life, her close friend had succumbed to breast cancer. This rocked Sarah's world and made her think about her marriage, which had drifted aimlessly for years. We explored Sarah's past and discovered that she was one of many people who wander along the marital path without ever reaching the enjoyment they desire.

She wanted to talk about her feelings before inviting her husband, Kelly, to attend a session. We discussed her journey to this point.

"Something is missing. We get along okay, but I want more in my marriage. I want to be really in love with him, but I am not sure that he wants the same. We talk about our problems, agree to make improvements, and then make little changes that don't seem to have any impact. We go away for a weekend once a year and go to a movie occasionally, but it just doesn't seem to be enough."

"Perhaps it isn't enough," I said. "Maybe you two need more than just a little change. Maybe you need to sit down and talk about making significant adjustments in how you relate. Having a night out once a month hardly sounds like a recipe for rekindling the romance in your relationship."

"Yeah, I guess you're right. He tends to put most of his energy into his work, while I devote my time to our kids and the house. We don't do a lot to keep the fires alive. A little here and a little there doesn't seem to add up to much. I keep thinking that a minor change here or there will make a difference, but it never seems to. When I've talked to Kelly about improving things, he acknowledges the problem and agrees to solutions, but he rarely follows through. I wonder what it's going to take."

"One of the biggest mistakes couples make is to be satisfied with minor adjustments that are not enough to create the results that both partners want. It's no different than what you confront while raising your kids. When you see your children making some poor decisions that seriously impact their lives, I doubt that a little talk changes things."

"I know what you mean. Changing a child's behavior takes more than talk. A little change doesn't cut it. I have to let them know what's at stake and make sure that they are buying into the changes that I want to see happen."

"Exactly. You have to paint a picture for them and help them see what you're trying to create. Then you have to make sure they are following the plan. That same dedication to change is needed with your husband."

"I guess I haven't done much to give him the message that a little change will not make things happen that I am imagining for us. He probably doesn't have a clue as to what my vision is for our marriage. I guess that's a place to start. I could tell him what I really want for us."

The Practice of Enrollment

Benjamin and Rosamund Zander have written a marvelous book titled *The Art of Possibility* in which they discuss the concept of *enrollment*.

> Enrollment is the art and practice of generating a spark of possibility for others to share....Our universe is alive with sparks. We have at our fingertips an infinite capacity to light a spark of possibility. Passion, rather than fear, is the igniting force. Abundance, rather than scarcity, is the context.[1]

They explain that in the Middle Ages, when starting a fire was a very difficult process, people carried a metal box containing a smoldering cinder. Imagine the possibilities if we carried with us an ember, ready to ignite others with the possibility of our vision. The practice of enrollment means that we take the responsibility for having a spark ready at all times. We carry with us the vision, the roadmap, for how we and those we love can arrive at a common destination together.

The Zanders list several steps to practicing enrollment:

- Imagine that people are an invitation for enrollment.
- Be ready to participate, willing to be moved and inspired.
- Offer that which lights you up.
- Have no doubt that others are eager to catch the spark.

You may be wondering just how excited your spouse is to catch the spark. Before limiting yourself with impossibility thinking, ask yourself how effectively you have shared the vision. Have you passed along the spark of passion about your desired destination? How vibrant is your enthusiasm?

If we lack enthusiasm and fail to share the vision, others will have no stake in it.

The Way to Transformation

A woman dreamed that she walked into a brand-new shop in the marketplace and, to her surprise, found God behind the counter.

"What do you sell here?" she asked.

"Everything your heart desires," said God.

Hardly daring to believe what she was hearing, the woman decided to ask for the best things a human could request.

"I want peace of mind and love and happiness and wisdom and freedom from fear," she said. Then, as an afterthought, she said, "Not just for me, but for everyone on earth."

God smiled. "I think you've got me wrong, my dear," He said. "We don't sell fruit here, only seeds."[2]

The story illustrates what we know to be true. We all have the ability to be transformed, but change only happens when we plant seeds and cultivate them. Sudden, miraculous changes are very rare. Just as the gardener lovingly and attentively tends her plants, so too we must watch over our desired areas of change. An inattentive eye will leave weeds that will crowd out the fledgling plants.

We may desire change, but we also fear it. We want so badly for things to be different, but at the same time we hope that things will not change too dramatically. We fear letting go, losing control. Because of these fears, most of us make progress in fits and spurts, lurching forward and then slipping backward. Not only do we fail to truly appreciate our ambivalence about change, as we have already seen, we also fail to take into consideration its full cost.

In order to move forward, we need to understand the difference between superficial change and transformation. Transformation is a radical alteration in our personality and nature. When we are transformed, we become new creatures. Such change is not light stuff.

The Scriptures talk about transformation in a way that is useful to our discussion. When Jesus spoke about the kingdom of God, He used many symbols of transformation:

• growing plants

- yeast in dough
- marriage
- birth
- fire, light, and wind

When the apostle Paul talked about transformation, he said, "If anyone is in Christ, he is a new creation; the old has gone, the new has come" (2 Corinthians 5:17).

In our quest to transform ourselves, we must allow God's healing to enter us fully. We know that when we try to change, we usually fail, but when we allow God to enter into us completely, we change.

When we allow God to do His work in us, we sometimes see immediate change. At other times we may not think anything is happening to us on the surface, but God is changing us deep within. The divine yeast is stirring us.

God offers us a new creation rather than superficial change. New growth from a deep center. When our inner selves waken, stretch, stand up, move out, and make choices, our terror of change becomes the hunger, thirst, and ecstasy of dynamic growth.

God's promise of transformation is not a demand to clean up our act. He will never threaten. God's promise is the ecstatic invitation of a lover to his beloved. *Come join yourself to me, and from our togetherness will come the new creation.*

One of the first signs of deep transformation is a strengthening of our sense of identity, the emergence of a more powerful self. This is not to be confused with selfishness. Selfish, ego-oriented people usually lack a strong sense of identity. Because they are so empty within, they grasp at anything they can to enhance their fragile sense of self. While many consider these kinds of people "full of them-selves," they are actually anything but full. They are painfully empty. A critical eye will see that and feel sadness for their insecurities.

A second sign of transformation occurs when we develop an increasing awareness of the needs of others. We have compassion for those around us. When we value other people for who they are, we are less likely to manipulate or misuse them. We appreciate them for all their beauty.

A third sign of transformation in the healed, revitalized personality is a change in values, priorities, and attitudes. We make different choices. We make decisions that reflect our new relationship with God, with others, and with ourselves.

Augustine said, "Love God and do as you like." This may sound surprisingly simple and perhaps even dangerous, but a deep love for God and relationship with Him changes us, and we desire to please Him.

I have found this prayer helpful in my life:

> God, if this action is right for me, let it grow and become more important and be firmly established in my life. If this is wrong, let it become less important and disappear from my life.

Making this prayer a habit and committing to it will gradually transform your life and your decisions. It will lessen your grip on things you may now believe to be important but may not be the best for you.

Cheryl and Kenneth

When Cheryl and Kenneth came to the couples' workshop sponsored by our church, their marriage needed a strong dose of vitality. They were similar to many other couples whose marriage suffers from entropy, a state of gradual decay or decline. The insidious corrosion was hardly noticeable at the time, but hindsight and reflection revealed the damage.

After 20 years together, Cheryl and Kenneth were ready for change. They had tried making minor corrections here and there without notable improvement. Each failed attempt to make progress only left them more discouraged. Their communication still lacked depth and intimacy, their love life was hollow and monotonous, their affection for one another waning. As they stared midlife in the eyes and watched their children leaving home, they knew their marriage needed an overhaul, not just a tune-up. They wanted transformation, not just superficial change.

They came up to me during a break between sessions and asked to talk. They briefly shared their story. High school sweethearts, they once had a passion that was electric. They became best friends and lovers. But responsibilities and benign neglect had taken their toll. They wanted to create something new and exciting. They were ready for transformation.

I was encouraged by their resolve. That was certainly the place to begin, I told them. They needed a new focus and new purpose regarding their marriage. They needed a new reason to be together. Staying together for the sake of the kids or because they had been married 20 years would certainly not transform their relationship.

I asked them to agree upon some new goals for their marriage. I encouraged them to let God be a healing influence in their relationship. I reminded them that rooted in God, they would find the sustenance to unselfishly love each other. And in God they would also find strength to be the people He created them to be. He would transform them as individuals and as a couple. We prayed together, and I sent them out to remake the vision for their marriage.

We met again later in the workshop. Both were smiling as they approached me, hand in hand. They had taken paper and pen and drafted a new map for their marriage. They had agreed upon new goals to strive for, new adventures to enjoy, and a new purpose for being together. Most important, they had agreed to make God the central focus of their lives, to let Him do some healing work in their marriage and in their individual lives. Cheryl and Kenneth were open to being transformed, not just changed on the outside.

The Lesson of Salt

In the Gospel of Matthew Jesus says, "You are the salt of the earth. But if the salt loses its saltiness, how can it be made salty again? It is no longer good for anything, except to be thrown out and trampled by men" (Matthew 5:13).

When exposed to certain elements, salt loses it potency. It loses its ability to enhance flavor. Jesus knew that we are like salt. We can maintain our ability to enhance the flavor of a relationship, or we can become leached out, bland, zestless.

Can you imagine a meal without salt? Without seasoning, many foods would taste bland. Like fine meals, marriages need salt. They need doses of adventure, excitement, and encouragement to keep them strong and vibrant. When things become bland, when the salt loses its saltiness, small changes do no good. The old salt must be thrown out. New salt must be found.

Perhaps that is where you are in your marriage today. Perhaps you have been trying to eat meals together without the proper seasoning. One meal tastes just like all of the others. The routines of marriage blur together, making one day indistinct from the last. Perhaps your salt has lost its potency. Transformation is still possible for you!

What Makes Him Tick?

Many people lose the ability to create positive change in their marriage. Their relationships are filled with good intentions, but good intentions are not enough. Men and women often begin a relationship with stars in their eyes and magic in the air. They are convinced nothing can make their relationship turn sour. But as we all know, new love can fade with time.

As John Gray noted, "With the best and most loving intentions love continues to die. Somehow the problems creep in. The resentments build. Communication breaks down. Mistrust increases. Rejection and repression result. The magic of love is lost."[3]

Men see a problem and fix it. But their focus is primarily on the outside world. They seem to have little time or tolerance for discussing problems in the family and marriage. They want answers that are quick and straight to the point. They do not want to look deeply into the heart of a matter.

Poet Robert Bly sees a deeper problem, one he has described as the "soft male." He writes: "Many of these men are unhappy: there's not much energy to them. They are life preserving but not exactly *life giving*. And why is it you often see these men with strong women who positively radiate energy?"[4]

Lulled into a sense of complacency, many women tolerate and perhaps even encourage this lack of focus and vibrancy. Women have long considered the home to be their domain. Our society has encouraged men to make their name in the world and rewarded them for doing so. Men do not aggressively cultivate the arts of communication and intimacy.

Many researchers, including John Gray, have noted that men's needs and women's needs are very different. These differences can eventually cause trouble. Gray lists male versus female needs.

Men:	Women:
• trust	• caring
• acceptance	• understanding
• appreciation	• respect
• admiration	• devotion
• approval	• validation
• encouragement	• reassurance[5]

A brief review of the list shows that a couple can get into trouble quickly if they are not tuned in to the other's love language. Unfortunately, many men neither take the time nor have the inclination to study the needs of their partner. They lope along, assuming that things in the home will take care of themselves if they tend to the world of work. Women should make sure their husbands understand that this will no longer sustain their marriage. A little change will not be sufficient to transform the marriage into a vital and verdant place where love can grow.

Now What?

As you proceed through this book, one secret builds upon another. You have begun to confront the lies that inhibit change and make your relationship stagnant. You are learning to cut through excuses and come out of hiding. In this chapter, you became aware that little changes are not enough to create the dynamic relationship that you seek.

Now you must continue along the path of true change, or deep transformation. You no longer accept cosmetic changes and will strive for those that are fundamental to your personality. You will be satisfied with nothing less than radical, dynamic transformation of your marriage. And, infused with clear focus, commitment, and the powerful help of God, you will find it.

Eight

Don't Be Afraid

*Serenity comes not alone by
removing the natural causes and
occasions of fear, but by the discovery
of inward reservoirs to draw upon.*

RUFUS M. JONES

She was an emergency room physician, capable of handling the most terrifying crises, situations most of us could never face. She did not know from one moment to the next if she would be dealing with a gunshot wound to the head or a patient with a knife lunging at her in a methamphetamine haze. She came to expect these kinds of situations, anesthetized to dangers that would leave a normal person cowering in fear. More than any of them would admit, she and her colleagues enjoyed the adrenaline-pumping action. This MASH-like training would serve her well in the days ahead.

She was not content to limit her work to emergency rooms. She sought even more adventure in Antarctica, a place many of us only read about in *National Geographic*. At the Amundsen-Scott South Pole Station, Dr. Jerri Nielsen served as the only physician to 41 scientists. She also faced the greatest challenge of her life. Already a veteran of years of horrific spousal abuse, isolated by her husband from family and friends and a survivor of a bitter divorce, she now stared dispassionately at a new threat that could easily claim her life. In the midst of this ordeal she maintained an inner reservoir of calm that helped her become a national hero.

Dr. Nielsen writes in her bestseller, *Ice Bound,* "My hair was long and blond when I arrived at the Pole, but now my head is completely bald, and coddled like an egg in a soft wool hat beneath my hood."[1] Exhibiting the bravery and stoicism typical of the other scientists, she hoped for months that the mass in her breast was a cyst and would shrink. It wasn't, and it didn't. Thousands of miles from the nearest state-of-the-art medical facility, she discovered that her body was racked with the symptoms of breast cancer. Isolated, alone, and dealing with changes in her body that she knew spelled danger, she was forced to make decisions we can only hope we never have to make. Amazingly, she was not afraid. "There was no way out. As medical officer, I knew better than anyone that in case of serious illness, we could depend only on our own scant resources. There was no way to evacuate the injured and no way to get more medication or equipment."[2] She diagnosed, biopsied, and treated her own breast cancer, and after the Air National Guard rescued her under perilous weather conditions, she returned to safety, an inspiration to all.

How did she acquire such resolve, courage, and strength? Is that same deep reservoir of resolve available to you and me? I believe it is. Our seventh secret for moving forward with your life is this: *You don't need to be afraid.*

Do you remember the story of the little engine that could?[3] The little engine, usually relegated to the mundane task of moving cars from one part of the yard to another, received a special assignment to deliver toys to the children over the mountain in the neighboring valley. The larger engines laughed at her because the trip required climbing up a steep mountainside before descending into the valley beyond. But the children were counting on her, and she wasn't going to let them down.

Each mile that passed became harder, and the little engine was afraid that she would fail. But as the climb got steeper, she told herself, *I think I can, I think I can...* Nearly out of steam, she finally reached the top and raced down the other side, telling herself, *I thought I could, I thought I could...*

Whether you are facing a crisis like Dr. Nielsen's, a marriage that needs transformation, or a situation that requires some extra encouragement, you do not need to be afraid. The powerful tools in this chapter can help you replace your paralyzing fear with encouragement and strength.

The Voices of Fear

In previous chapters, we have confronted lies that keep you from growing. You have begun to enlarge your world. Perhaps you are expanding your options and finding new ways to talk to your partner. Most importantly, you should be discovering new ways of talking to yourself. When the lies disappear, new and powerful truths emerge.

Fear whispers lies to us.

- You should be careful, or you'll make a big mistake.
- Your problems are your fault, and you should be ashamed.
- This is the best that it can get, so be quiet and accept things.
- You could make matters much worse if you take action.

You may have a chorus of troublesome, threatening voices. They would keep you stuck, but you need to be free to make new choices. And new choices are available to you. Remember that FEAR means False Evidence Appearing as Real!

Fear lurks not only in diabolically destructive and abusive relationships but also in most "normal" marriages. It is a companion to most of us.

If you never feel fear, check to see if you are still breathing. You might have felt fears as a child in your home. Even if your family looked good from the outside, a closer look might have revealed circumstances that you did not want others to see. You may have had a mother or father who planted seeds of fear. You may have cringed in the corner of your room when you heard your parents fighting, wondering when the violence would end. Maybe you were the victim of the abuse. Or perhaps you were the one who jumped into the middle of the fray, trying to bring a bit of sanity to the situation.

People with a "normal" childhood also struggle with fear. Perhaps adult life has been more than you had imagined, and its stresses and challenges overwhelm you. You may wonder why life is so difficult at times and why you cannot simply be happier. Fears are not always easily attached to one event or problem. You may clear away one problem only to find another.

Fear continues to be an issue in the lives of many—and in many Christian marriages. We would like to believe that all Christian marriages are free from issues of abuse of power and control, but this is not the case. Many individuals in Christian marriages struggle with a variety of fears.

We do not experience fear in the same way or with the same intensity. Though a fear may seem irrational to us, it can be a powerful force in someone else's life. For example, many commonly fear change, even change for the better. We cling tenaciously to that which we know even if it is not best for us.

Many also fear making a mistake. They wonder what will happen if they make a change in their life and then things turn out to be worse. What will they do then? And what if the changes they make lead to consequences they had not anticipated? We tend to hold fast to the world that we know and are comfortable with. In a marriage that has many good qualities as well as bad, we may be inclined to settle for the bad because we do not know what will happen if we risk making changes. Indeed, fear paralyzes.

Lots of people avoid talking to their spouses about sensitive issues because they fear the confrontation that will ensue. For many, the fear of confrontation brings cold sweats and a desire to run for cover. Perhaps you can relate to those who would rather walk across hot coals than face an angry man ready for confrontation.

People in unhappy marriages may also be afraid of how their spouse will make them feel. A wife may be afraid that her husband will turn all of the problems on her and withdraw his love and approval. If she is dependent upon that love and approval for her self-worth, which is very common, she will feel like she is on an emotional roller coaster. If she fears him withdrawing his love and approval, she may be willing to do just about anything to keep it, even suffer through a great deal of pain.

A client named Terri described living in fear of her husband's disapproval.

"I remember how it was for me to be so wrapped up in making sure Jim agreed with everything I was doing. I used to tiptoe around him, changing my behavior to please him. It was like he became my little god. I was embarrassed at how much power he had over me. I grew up afraid of my stepfather, and I think I transferred a lot of those feelings over to Jim. It wasn't that Jim was totally controlling. I had just learned that I was supposed to please a man no matter what, and I should never make him angry. It took me a long time to understand that I would never be happy unless I was content to just be myself."

Women are often afraid that men will make them feel bad. Too often, men don't stop at withdrawing their love and approval. They are often masters at manipulating women to get them to do what they want. Men often want women to be available at their beck and call to attend to their needs. They like nurturance and dislike conflict. They want someone who will generally agree with them and make them feel good.

Women are also afraid of the way men might behave. Even if you state your opinion in a respectful manner, he may still get angry. He may become belligerent, rant, rave, and be unhappy. He may try a variety of tactics until he finds out that these methods will not make you swallow your feelings. He may resort to threats or may withdraw into silence. In any of these situations, you must believe from the outset that you do not need to be afraid. You can make choices to be safe and still retain the integrity of your marriage. This will take inner resolve and a clear purpose, but you can do it.

Susan Jeffers, author of the popular book *Feel the Fear and Do It Anyway,* explains that many fears have to do with inner states of mind rather than external situations. She says, "They reflect your sense of self and your ability to handle this world. This explains why generalized fear takes place. If you are afraid of being rejected, this fear will affect almost every area of your life—friends, intimate relationships, job interviews, and so on. Rejection is rejection—wherever it is found. So you begin to protect yourself and, as a result, greatly limit yourself. You begin to shut down and close out the world around you."[4]

What Jeffers is saying is that even though many situations arouse fear in us, most of the fear that we experience has to do with the voices in our own heads. It has to do with old messages that we have repeated thousands of times but have never held up to close scrutiny. We thoroughly rehearse our fears and devote too little energy to combating them with the truth.

Sandy and Ted

Sandy was a middle-aged woman who came to see me after struggling with a debilitating marital separation. She had not wanted the separation, and it had taken its toll on her. The first few months of the separation had been excruciating. Hardly able to sleep or eat, she found some assistance from medications that seemed to take the edge off her pain.

Sandy had been a fearful woman even before she and Ted separated, and this tragedy seemed to awaken old fears. Her parents had taught her to always be cautious, but being cautious had not prevented her husband from leaving. Afraid of being alone, she had begged Ted to stay, but she could not convince him. Nor could she stop him from talking about a divorce, in spite of pleas from her pastor, their friends, and herself. He wanted some space to think about their relationship. He said that the issues were not just about her and that he still loved her, but she still blamed herself. She was scared to death that he might end their marriage.

Sandy struggled to find a way to live with their separation without panic. She hated living in limbo, but she wanted to show Ted that she could be strong and make some of the personal changes she felt he wanted for their marriage. She wanted to learn to take more chances and to be open to more adventure, which seemed to be one of the major issues lacking for him in their marriage. She wanted to learn to enjoy travel and perhaps to take dancing lessons instead of hiding at home so often. But she was fighting old ghosts, old ways of behaving she had learned as a child. She was trying to live down old messages about her self-worth that only worsened in their marriage.

As we talked, Sandy clearly had many old messages to review. She had learned long ago

- She must always be careful.
- Life is filled with scarcity rather than abundance.
- She must not make mistakes.
- She should never make others unhappy with her.
- She is powerless to change her life.

We looked closely at these messages, how they made her feel about herself, and how they influenced her interactions with her husband. She looked closely at her tendency to stifle her opinions in their marriage and even with their children. She was not responsible for his choice to move out, but she could see that she had played a role in his decision. She worked hard to ferret out her anger at him for abandoning her. She began to understand his decision to create some space in the hope that significant change would occur.

Through months of hard work in counseling, Sandy was able to move beyond some of the destructive childhood beliefs that had made her world so small. She made remarkable changes, and her husband noticed. She went back to college to finish her baccalaureate degree and is working toward obtaining her teaching credentials, something she had wanted to do for a long time. She took risks by changing her hairstyle and buying new clothes, adding to her positive feelings about herself. She began asserting herself more with her husband and strengthened her voice with their grown children. She started feeling better about herself and increasing the possibilities for their marriage.

At this time Ted and Sandy are seeing one another and have hopes for their marriage. He has noticed her changes, and she feels much more confident about herself and their marriage. Not all of their issues are resolved, but they are both very hopeful about the changes they have made.

Antidotes to Fear

Fear paralyzes, but truth frees. Truth opens an exciting world of hope and promise. It allows you to see yourself and your place in the world in new and electrifying ways. One of the powerful choices you are free to make is to voice what is true for you. You are free to explain how you feel when something threatens you. Your husband may not intend his words or actions to be threatening, but if you feel threatened, you are free to talk about it. However, you are only free to voice what is true for you, not what you believe is true for him. The difference is critical. We are never able to read another person's mind, intentions, or motivations, and to attempt to do so only breeds resentment.

You are also free to make decisions that help you feel safe. At times that may simply mean setting boundaries for your personal well-being. You may choose not to go to the company picnic. You may choose not to have the whole family over for Thanksgiving as you did last year. You may choose not to have sex if the emotional climate is not suitable for doing so. You can make choices to lessen your fears and strengthen your personal sense of well-being.

You are also free to use your intuition to make decisions. While this attribute is dismissed by some, I suspect it is a larger part of our world than we might admit. Certainly it seems to be a powerful source of information for many people, and you may do well to listen to it. It can be very tuned in to the work of the Holy Spirit in your life. Listening to yourself can undoubtedly enhance your ability to sense God's direction and see His work in your life.

Jeffers shares a number of additional truths that will make your world larger and more invigorating.

Fear will never go away as long as I continue to grow. She notes that as long as we push out into our world in new ways, we will experience discomfort. If we wait for the fear to go away before we try new things, we will wait forever. Complete comfort only comes to those who live stagnant lives. And even though we would rather not admit it, stagnant lives become uncomfortable at some point as well.

The only way to get rid of the fear of doing something is to go out and do it. Jeffers says that the "doing it" comes *before* the fear goes away. I was invited recently to go flying with a friend in what I call a "puddle jumper." This bucket of bolts seemed to be held together with chewing gum and bailing wire, and I was not particularly anxious to leave the ground with him. But I did not want to be limited by my fears, and I have recently been pushing myself in new ways. Seizing the opportunity to go flying on that beautiful day, I went up in spite of my fears. To be honest, I was afraid during much of the flight. But fear usually dissipates the longer we stay in a troubling situation, so I went flying a second time a few days later in hopes of fully allaying my fears. The second time was easier, as was the third.

The only way to feel better about myself is to go out and do what I've been afraid to do. Again, doing it comes before feeling better about it. When we push forward in spite of our fears, not only do our fears fade but our self-esteem grows as well. What a nice bonus! If you tackle new things in your life, you will feel less fear. As you feel less fear, you will be willing to tackle more things. And so it goes.

I am not the only one who experiences fear in unfamiliar territory. So does everyone else. We are funny people. We are so tempted to think that we are the only ones feeling inadequate and fearful. We think we are the only ones going through relationship crises or struggling with finances. Naturally egocentric, we forget that others struggle with similar issues. We are not alone, and this knowledge should give us a bit of relief from our suffering.

I am always surprised to read about Hollywood stars who are scared to death every time they must audition for a new film role. How can they be so frightened? They have chosen acting as their life's profession and have auditioned many times. Then I remember we all have our areas of difficulty.

I am frightened every time I must be an expert witness in the courtroom. I go through a very predictable cycle. First, I am excited to be asked to testify, and I enjoy meeting with attorneys in preparation for the trial. I like reading up on the case and preparing my answers to the questions I think the attorneys will ask. But as the date nears, I go through my fear phase. I wonder whether I will unravel in the courtroom, and I fear appearing to be the inadequate psychologist I sometimes believe myself to be. Finally, when I am on the witness stand, I feel a surge of excitement as I provide information about a topic with which I am familiar and passionate. After I testify, I feel relief and the satisfaction of a job well done.

Why do I put myself through such an ordeal? Why not just avoid putting myself on the line in front of colleagues whose opinions of me matter? That question has no easy answer. But I do know that the fear is manageable, and the payoffs are worth the risks.

Pushing through fear is less frightening than living with the feeling of helplessness. Jeffers now pushes us way out of our comfort zone with this last truth. She is saying that we all know that we will eventually have to face our fears. Somewhere, sometime, a day of reckoning will arrive. We will be forced to deal directly with death, the loss of a spouse, or the loss of a job. We have no control over many situations. To pretend that we do is to live in fantasyland, and that is not a healthy place to be. We are better off facing our fears and gaining some mastery over situations, knowing that we are stronger and more capable of handling similar situations in the future.[5]

Who, Me?

Another error we often make is assuming that the giants of our faith had no fears. We erroneously believe that their faith conquered all their fears and that they lived blissfully in the shadow of God's protection. As the story of Moses reveals, this could not be further from the truth.

As we read about the life of Moses and his repeated encounters with the Pharaoh of Egypt and with his own people, we see his persistent reluctance to be a leader. When God calls him, Moses says, "Who am I, that I should go to Pharaoh and bring the Israelites out of Egypt?" (Exodus 3:11). He later moans about his lack of authority, fear of people's distrust in him, speech difficulties, and sheer cowardice.

Moses does not complain once or twice but many times. He begs God to let him off the hook. After complaining of being "slow of speech and tongue" and having "faltering lips," he pleads with the Lord, "O Lord, please send someone else to do it" (Exodus 4:13). In spite of Moses' emotional meltdown, God says that He will be with Moses and assures him that he *can* do the job. Moses' example gives us hope that we can work through our fears and come out on the other side. We can move from feelings of inadequacy to confidence, but we will need God's help to do so.

A short time later, God says, "See, I have made you like God to Pharaoh, and your brother Aaron will be your prophet. You are to say everything I command you, and your brother Aaron is to tell Pharaoh to let the Israelites go out of his country" (Exodus 7:1-2). And the rest is history. Moses became a mighty leader, strengthened beyond his natural capabilities. Moses, Dr. Nielsen, and even the little engine that could remind us that bravery is not the absence of fear, but our actions in the face of our fears.

Jennifer

Jennifer was a young woman who came to see me rather urgently because she wanted her boyfriend to be more committed to their relationship. She had come out of a troubled engagement to another man a few years earlier, and now she thought she had found the right man. She had been with him over a year, enjoyed their relationship immensely, and was ready to move things forward. But he was reluctant to commit himself, and the more he resisted, the more frightened she became. Every time the topic of engagement or marriage came up, he would say that he was not ready for that kind of discussion, and she would go into an emotional tailspin. Jennifer was heartbroken on more than one occasion.

She had made this appointment with me after being unable to sleep restfully or eat for several days. She told me, "I ache for him. I can't think of anything else but him. All I want is to be with him. Sometimes I tell myself that I can live without his commitment, but then I obsess about it."

Clearly Jennifer struggles with far more than what we see on the surface. She wants what she cannot have. She undoubtedly loves this man but also has some dependency issues she must face. She must also face the fact that unfortunately, he is unwilling to commit himself to her. Any efforts she makes to force the issue are doomed to backfire. He may be asking himself if he wants to be with someone long-term who is so desperate and dependent.

Jennifer worked hard in counseling and was able to extricate herself from her entanglement with her boyfriend. She was able to pull back and give him space to decide what he wanted from their relationship. As is often the case, when she became more grounded within herself and content to live without him, the more interest he showed in the relationship. She did not rush back to him, however. First, she had to face other issues from her past that needed resolution before she could be emotionally available to him. She had to face other insecurities about her self-image that were exacerbated in a relationship.

Jennifer's struggles illustrate other truths we know about fear. Renowned expert Gavin De Becker, author of *The Gift of Fear*, says, "Fear summons powerful predictive resources that tell us what might come next. It is that which might come next that we fear—what *might* happen, not what is happening now."[6] Jennifer was not so much afraid of what was happening now as she was of what might happen next. She feared her boyfriend would be unwilling to commit himself. Even worse, she believed he might abandon her for someone else.

De Becker adds another insight into fear that applied to Jennifer. He noted that fear is rarely about what you think you fear but rather what you link to the current fear. He encourages us to think about the possible outcomes that we might fear. Jennifer's fears are deeper than she realizes. She may fear abandonment, being forever alone, or possible embarrassment and shame over another broken relationship. These are all issues for her to explore in counseling.

What Makes Him Tick?

Perhaps contemporary notions about men are right. We long to be "wild at heart," and we have a secret desire to be a combination of John Wayne, Sylvester Stallone, and Arnold Schwarzenegger, with a little Mel Gibson thrown in. We want to live daring lives, challenging ourselves and going where others don't dare. We want to compete against the odds and win the admiration of our beloved. And we want to know that we can hold our own against the competition as well. Secretly, we are still playing our own version of "king of the mountain," watching over our shoulders to see exactly where we stand.

Where does this take us in a relationship? We want a partner who is willing to forget the dirty diapers and parent-teacher meetings on occasion, to leave home and office work behind, as important as these are to family life. We want a mate who is willing to forget practical obligations and sail away with us on a passionate voyage to the South Seas. Hang the bills, forget practicality, dream big, if only for a short, dizzy season. We want spice in our lives and will go to great lengths to find it.

And what woman doesn't also want to be carried away from responsibility to a luxurious destination, free from worry? Are men the only ones who want to be daring? I don't think so. In fact, I believe that many women want to be whisked away to another land. But they need help getting there, and that is where men fail to fully appreciate the dilemma.

The trick is for both to face their fear of adventure and impracticality and let youthful fun and zest find a place in their marriage alongside the practicalities of family life. Both want the same thing, and if they will talk about it, make plans for it, and move in that direction, they will be happier for it.

Now What?

Ridding your life of the fear that paralyzes you is probably the most important issue in this book. Each secret has been designed to allow you to live life more fully, more completely, more in tune with yourself. Fear robs you of that possibility. Facing the fear that robs us of our vitality is one of the most critical issues in our lives.

This chapter has focused on letting go of fears, but we should respect our fears as well. A favorite author of mine, Harriet Goldhor Lerner, has written many books for women. In her book, *The Dance of Deception*, she reminds women to honor their fears. She eloquently summarizes what this chapter is about and what I hope for you.

> We need to respect our anxiety and pay attention to what our bodies are trying to tell us through it. But we don't have to succumb to fear. Fear is women's worst enemy. And it is not by accident that we are taught to fear. Fear serves to paralyze us, hold us in place, sap our energy and attention from important work, and limit our creativity and imagination. Fear keeps us close to home. It silences us. And if we wait until we are unafraid, or fixed, or analyzed, we may have waited too long.[7]

Nine

Your Inner Voice

To believe your own thought, to believe that what is true for you in your private heart is true for all men—that is genius.

RALPH WALDO EMERSON

At first I was disappointed to see another overcast day as I glanced out onto the water in front of my home. A soup-like fog rolled across the steel gray bay. But as I studied the mysterious clouds suspended over the water, I was intrigued to see the different shades of blue they painted on the fluid landscape. Sunlight shone through the fog, yielding another texture. Clouds, water, light, and wind all blended together to create a moving pastiche of color. If I looked closely enough, I found plenty to delight the eye. The beauty was all there for the taking, but I had to be intentional about seeking it.

Perhaps that is the way of the inner voice as well. It is that small part of us that knows what it knows, sees what it sees, and can understand what is real. If it is silenced for too long by banks of emotional fog, its muffled tones can become indistinguishable. So many winds of expectations, so many clouds of confusion, so much noise that drowns out our embryonic voice. So many people tugging at us to become what they want us to be, and then—one thought at a time, one word at a time—our voice is lost.

People who have lost their voice are wise to embark upon a journey to find it. And, having found it, to use it. That is the invitation of our eighth secret: *Find your inner voice and use it.* Realizing who we are, who God has made us to be, makes us strong. It is part of growing into our true selves.

Recently I heard a truism offered by "Dr. Phil" that I thought was apropos. Someone asked me a question, and I told her that I didn't know the answer. She retorted, "Well, you know what Dr. Phil would say? 'If you say you don't know something, it means you're not thinking.'"

Certainly those words contain some truth. When I say, "I don't know" these days, I ask myself whether I truly do not know or am simply taking the easy way out by saying I do not know. Usually I don't want to expend the energy to explore my thinking, or perhaps I want to keep my thoughts to myself. Either way, the result is that I silence my inner voice. To risk sharing what I think about the topic at hand is much more powerful. It is also much more demanding.

To contemplate what is going on inside of me takes work. For me, it does not come naturally. Consider how often one hears the words, "I don't know" when someone is asked a question. Could they truly not know what they think? Have they become a *human doing* for so long that to become a *human being* takes extra effort?

The world is an overwhelming cacophony. To stop and listen can be trying. One cannot even drive a car in silence anymore. We are assaulted by loud tailpipes, radios, and CD players pounding out their bass lines from cars that literally rock with the vibrations. Noise dominates our society so completely that we struggle to find a place to hear ourselves think.

But I wonder if we really want to hear ourselves think. I wonder if slowing down and listening to the inner musings of our hearts is too painful. A friend recently told me that she always keeps the television on to keep herself company. The voices on the tube keep her from feeling too lonely. How many of us have resorted to images of people on a screen to entertain us and keep us from becoming acquainted with ourselves?

If you are willing and brave, you can use this secret to gain freedom in your life. You will have to put up with some risk and perhaps a little discomfort at first. But if you are willing to embark on the inward journey, you will find your inner voice and use it.

Just Pretending

When I was a child I spent much of my time in a fantasy world. I wasn't trying to escape the threatening realities of human experience. I just liked living in a more exciting world.

Pretending can be a playful form of creativity. Such was the case when a group of us boys pretended to be Daniel Boone and Davy Crockett. We wore our coonskin caps and were armed with knives, bows, and arrows. (We sometimes switched roles and became Indians on the warpath.) In this world of make-believe, we could try out different aspects of bravery we did not yet possess in real life. We could imagine the thrill of saving a town from imminent destruction and rescuing its citizens from injury and death.

A few years later I entered another imaginary world. Motivated by the television show *The Man From U.N.C.L.E.,* a friend and I wrote scripts that always involved the same plot: Hero saves civilization from evil conspiracy. I was the hero, of course, and my skills were limited only by my imagination.

Today we commonly see hero worship in full force. Advertising executives play on this phenomenon. We see children who "want to be like Mike" so much that we can't walk down the street without seeing someone wearing

Air Jordans. I understand. Wearing the shoes helps kids imagine the feeling of sailing through the air and finishing an acrobatic slam dunk like Michael Jordan.

And girls have their own cult heroes. The latest seems to be Brittany Spears, though by the time this book hits the press, another will likely have captured the hearts of young people. As I did as a child, they want to escape their own world, which they may perceive as limited and limiting, and enter a place filled with possibility.

Escapism and hero worship are certainly not all bad. In fact, they can inspire us to move beyond our limitations and enter a larger world of possibility. This pretending can be a powerful motivator that encourages the average athlete to excel, the poor student to earn better grades, the struggling vocalist to reach for seemingly unreachable notes. Pretending can lift us higher, and encourage us to be stronger and wiser. But pretending has its pitfalls. When taken to unhealthy limits, it can result in the loss of our true voice.

Pretending as Deception

Pretending can also be a dangerous venture, as is illustrated by Harriet Goldhor Lerner in her book *The Dance of Deception.* She reminds us that many use pretending to cope with difficulties, and using deception is a common occurrence. For example, pretending to be innocent of wrongdoing when in fact you are guilty can save you from additional embarrassment and public humility. Pretending to be asleep when an abusive stepfather comes into your room in the middle of the night can save you from emotional and physical trauma.

In a more innocuous vein, many of us pretend not to be home when a friend calls and asks if we are busy, perhaps because we may not be up to the strain of entertaining guests at that moment. Or we may pretend to know something that we in fact do not know to avoid embarrassment. The line between pretending and lying can easily turn to a blur. Goldhor notes:

> Whether the intention is to dazzle or distract, confuse or camouflage, masquerade or malinger, impress or impersonate, pretending is an ever-present adaptation strategy throughout all nature....The human capacity to hide the real and display the false is truly extraordinary, allowing us to regulate relationships through highly complex choices about how we present ourselves to others.[1]

Melissa's Lost Voice

Melissa came to see me at the request of her physician. A heavyset, 36-year-old woman, casually dressed, she made an immediate impression. She was rather abrupt, asking questions about my office policy and making critical comments about my office staff. I became tense and wondered what might be troubling her.

She sat down and immediately made sure I knew that she did not need to be there. Her voice was laced with hostility as if I had forced her to come and tell her story. I asked her why her doctor suggested a visit to a psychologist.

She told me that she felt our meeting was a waste of time but respected her doctor and promised him to attend one session. She would not be returning, she said. I clearly had my work cut out for me.

"So," I said. "Do you have any idea why your doctor suggested you come and see me?"

"I don't know. I don't think any of this is necessary."

"Perhaps you are right. But why don't we make the best of it and talk a bit."

"What do you want to know?"

"Tell me about your visits with your doctor, and what kinds of physical problems you are having."

"I don't really see the relevance of it, but all right. I have periodic bouts of ulcerative colitis. He thinks that the flare-ups may be related to something happening at home or at work."

"How long have you been struggling with the colitis?"

"For about the last two years. Ever since I took over as account executive at my work."

"Any other significant changes in your life in the past year or two?"

"Yes. I got married and moved here. I lived in Houston for ten years. It's been a little hectic."

"It sounds to me like you've been through some major changes. What do you do to let off steam from your job and the other pressures in your life?"

"I don't have much time to pamper myself after working all day and taking care of my responsibilities at home."

"So how are you and your husband doing?"

"We've done better, but I don't think it's anything to be concerned about. Just typical tensions that come from all the stress we've been under. Nothing we need professional help to deal with."

Melissa's defensiveness made me wary about pushing her. She intended to keep her privacy, and revealing areas of inner vulnerability to a person she did not know or trust was not something she could do easily. Yet her physical condition was clearly tied to emotional problems. She would not be able to hear that today, however. My goal was to gain her trust so that she could open up about her feelings as we progressed.

When the session ended, Melissa reluctantly agreed to return. She lowered her guard and slowly revealed more of her struggles. In the weeks that followed, she shared that as the oldest of five children, she had learned to take care of others and avoid any sign of weakness. She had learned to gain recognition by being a perfectionist and excelling in everything she did. She had learned to hide away her feelings and always pretend that things were fine. Leaning on others had never been an option, so sharing her true self with me was a major undertaking.

Melissa spent the next few months telling me about her painful childhood. She shared about her difficult years in a stepfamily and her relentless push to be the best in everything she undertook. She stopped at nothing short of perfection, and her stomach kept score. She demanded the same level of performance from her husband, and he was beginning to buckle under the strain. Their relationship was not going well, and she knew that much of their struggle had to do with her critical, demanding nature. She discovered that there was a little girl inside that still longed for approval and acceptance. The hard-driving, businesslike façade was a cover for a frightened child who wanted someone to accept her for who she was. She shared her deep desire that people respect her unique strengths and traits. She was tired of constantly pushing to accomplish more.

Melissa had come to believe in her own façade. She had hidden her true feelings from others and even from herself. She had come to believe that everything would be fine if she worked hard and demanded perfection from herself and others. She had given up her inner voice long ago and learned to play a role. The no-nonsense, no-vulnerability approach helped her survive her childhood and excel in the business world but ignored the girl within that wanted love and acceptance from her husband and others.

Keri's Lost Voice

Melissa had lost her voice to a tougher, more powerful façade, but Keri's plight was quite different. She had lost her voice to silence. She had grown up in a family that lived by an unspoken rule: Don't talk about your feelings or speak against your parents. We have enough problems to deal with.

Keri was an astute observer of family dynamics. Watching her parents fight continuously, she decided early on that she would play the role of "the good girl." Her older brothers got into trouble with the law, but she made her parents proud by being good. They had enough problems of their own, struggling to save their marriage and solve her brothers' legal problems. She kept a low profile and simply faded into the woodwork.

She came to counseling voluntarily when her depression became unmanageable. She had perfected the art of hiding so completely that instead of sharing her opinion, she always deferred to others. She was always sweet, but secretly came to hate that description of her demeanor. Still, she acted the part until she was nearly ready to explode.

Keri had no idea why she was depressed. She insisted that her marriage was wonderful, her job was enjoyable, and her relationships with her children and friends were all quite normal. She finally told me of her recurring nightmares in which her parents fought and she hid in her closet to muffle the noise. Those experiences were in the past, she insisted. She was not convinced they had any bearing upon her life today.

As her counseling progressed, Keri began to see that she had lost her voice long ago. At work she was always cooperative, never expressing a contrary point of view. With her parents, she was still the doting daughter, always offering assistance whenever they called on her, always submitting to their demands even when it meant she had to give up a part of herself to do so. In her marriage she stifled all her anger. She was the dutiful woman she read about in Proverbs 31— the wife of noble character.

But where was the real Keri? How could she rediscover her inner nature? What would have to happen before she was willing to come out and voice her preferences? After a lot of work, she began to see that she could express her opinions and even disagree with people without being obstructive or oppositional. She could state a contrary point of view without being rebellious. And, despite what she had been told as a child, speaking up did not automatically create turmoil for those around her. But old rules and ways of behaving are hard to recognize and even harder to give up.

Keri and Melissa both worked hard to find their inner voice. They did their best to:

- identify their real feelings
- understand and accept their feelings
- compare and contrast their beliefs with those around them
- honor their beliefs as valuable, distinct, and worthy of being heard
- state their beliefs openly
- be comfortable disagreeing with others
- ask for what they needed

Keri gradually came to see that silence served no purpose. It was not mandated in the Bible, and it was not what God intended for her life. It was merely a mechanism she had clung to as a way of coping with her dysfunctional family. It was a worn-out way of being and believing. It added to her depression and limited the quality of her marriage and family life.

Finding Your True Face

Finding and using your true *voice* will be much easier once you have become comfortable with your true *face*. What is the difference? Very little, and a lot.

Your true voice is that unique and authentic inner voice that whispers your truth to you. That voice distinguishes what you believe from what others believe or think. Your true face is the image that is consistent with your true voice, your true self.

However, your true face may not be the one you project to the world. In fact, you may not even recognize your true face because you have worn a different face for so long. This face is often an imposter, posing as the real you when in fact it is not. However, when you play a role so often and with so much intensity, ending that role and finding and living out your true face can be very difficult.

We become invested in this image that we present to the world. We project to others what we want them to see. Before long, we start believing that *we are that role*. We develop a voice that matches our role, and we begin to lose our true voice.

Robert Wicks, author of the wonderful book *Touching the Holy*, tells a delightful story that illustrates this lesson:

> The Iroquois Indians tell a fascinating story of a strange and unusual figure they call the Peacemaker. The Peacemaker came to a village where the chief was known as The Man Who Kills and Eats People. Now The Man Who Kills and Eats People was in his wigwam. He had cut up his enemies and was cooking them in a massive pot in the center of the wigwam so that he might eat them and absorb their mythical powers.
>
> The Peacemaker climbed to the top of the wigwam and looked down through the smoke hole, and his face was reflected in the grease on the top of the pot. The Man Who Kills and Eats People looked into the pot, saw the Peacemaker's reflection, and thought it to be his own face.
>
> And he said: "Look at that. That's not the face of a man who kills his enemies and eats them. Look at the nobility. Look at the peace in that face. If that is my face, what am I doing carrying on this kind of life?"
>
> And he seized the pot, dragged it from the fire, brought it outside and poured it on the ground. He then called the people and said: "I shall never again take the life of an enemy. I shall never again destroy

or consume an enemy, for I have discovered my true face. I have found out who I am."

Then the Peacemaker came down from the top of the wigwam and embraced him and called him Hiawatha.[2]

Wicks goes on to say:

If we are able to see our "true face" reflected in the loving eyes of God in prayer and in the faces of those who love us unconditionally, we ultimately then feel the confidence to see our own errors and shortcomings in a different way....People who know themselves and are at peace with themselves have something to share—no matter how difficult the situation turns out to be.[3]

The Fuel for Change

Emotion has rightfully been called "energy in motion." It is the fuel used to change situations. You may recall that Christ exhibited the full range of emotions and shared them openly. He grieved at the death of His friend Lazarus, He became angry with the sellers in the temple and drove them out, He was impatient with His disciples for their lack of understanding, He was sorrowful on the cross as He lamented to the Father. In each situation His emotion led Him to a certain action or way of seeing things.

Just as Christ had emotions that became energy in motion, we have emotions that may lead us in valuable directions, or may be suppressed and create turmoil for us. God never intended for us to worship our emotions, but they are part of our unique identity and distinguish us from others.

Anger is one emotion worthy of special mention, for it is a potent fuel for change. As Julia Cameron states in *The Artist's Way*,

> Anger is meant to be listened to. Anger is a voice, a shout, a plea, a demand. Anger is meant to be respected....Anger is meant to be acted upon. It is not meant to be acted out. Anger points the direction. We are meant to use anger as fuel to take actions we need to move where anger points us. With a little thought, we can usually translate the message that our anger is sending us.[4]

If suppressed, our anger can develop into depression—anger turned inward. Acted out, anger can be destructive and hurtful to those around us. But used as fuel for change, anger can be a powerful and productive emotion.

Consider any anger you may be feeling, as well as its source. How might you constructively use your anger to enhance a troubled relationship? How might you be hiding your true feelings from your spouse, and what effect is that having on your relationship? Here is valuable fuel for change to improve your life and your primary relationships. Here is a way to claim a voice that you may have silenced long ago.

Hiding Our Talents

Every family gathering and workplace meeting needs to include the viewpoints of every member. The silent life is a hidden and wasted life. We should not hide our talents or our voices. Even dissention, though perhaps disliked in certain gatherings, can enhance the overall quality of a meeting. As someone once said, "If we are all in agreement, then we are not all needed here." Contrary points of view, shared in the right spirit, add spice to the life of the group.

A favorite writer of mine, Elizabeth O'Connor, spent years developing innovative programs at The Church of the Savior in Washington, D.C. In her book *The Eighth Day of Creation,* she draws an application from the parable of the talents. In this parable, the Lord tells of a man who was going into a foreign country and called together his servants. He loaned them money to invest while he was away. He gave varying amounts to each of the servants but expected each to use his money wisely. When he returned home, he discovered that one servant had dug a hole in the ground to hide the money for safekeeping. In essence he had hidden his voice, played it safe, and lived the unfulfilled life (Matthew 25:14-30). O'Connor calls him...

> ...the slothful servant who, receiving the one talent from his master, wraps it "in a clean white napkin" and buries it until he is called upon for an accounting. He plays safe and so forfeits that which was originally given. Similarly in life one may hoard a chosen virtue, running no risk of losing it through life experience that may require encountering evil within oneself or risking its loss in the marketplace of life. Too late, perhaps, we discover that what we have saved through false caution we have most truly lost.[5]

O'Connor goes on to challenge each of us to be who God calls us to be. She believes that Mathew 25 illustrates this principle as well. She goes on to say, "We may plead unconsciousness, yet, if we look back with honesty, we know that at a critical moment, an experience, a dream, or a voice came to arouse a consciousness of a new life which we refused."[6]

What might O'Connor say to us about our voice? I suspect she would challenge us to be completely true to our self. That one and only self that we have been given, that we work at growing into, is more than a gift. It is a responsibility that God has given to us. He calls us to live it fully, not squander it. We are not to silence ourselves nor be silenced. Our voice must be heard.

What Makes Him Tick?

As women seek to find their voice and use it, they can expect to run into men who will shout their affirmation and then, perhaps unconsciously, run for the hills. They will want their partner to be strong, lively, and verbal. Just not too much. Why? A woman who is capable of speaking her mind is very threatening for most men.

You are undoubtedly aware that our society considers men who are dominant in the business world to be capable, but it perceives women who are equally dominant and powerful as domineering and heartless. For all of our rhetoric to the contrary, I believe that men really struggle with a woman who is able to handle herself in male-dominated settings.

I would like to think all of this is changing. I am not completely convinced, however. I suspect that many men want their spouses to have self-confidence but not question them in their decisions. They want their partner to bring home a nice salary but also to make sure the laundry is done and supper is on the table. They want their spouse to be able to get her own car to the shop for repairs, but they also expect to have the final say in decisions pertaining to family life.

Yes, men are confused about what they want from women. But lest we poke fun at men too quickly, some of the same contradictions reside within women as well.

Bestselling author Susan Jeffers, in her book *Opening Our Hearts to Men*, says that women give men mixed signals too. She suggests that women, as well as men, fear intimacy and create barriers to it. Among other things, she says women...

- create barriers to intimacy
- are not open to men the way they are to women
- don't always want to hear the truth
- prefer closed men and choose them accordingly
- are too frightened of losing their identity to risk intimacy
- talk too much
- don't recognize men's attempts to connect with women.[7]

For all of their attempts at understanding women, men obviously struggle in this area. They have a hard time understanding the polarities that exist within the sexes, including tendencies to be both secure and insecure, loving and hateful, scared and confident, cold and warm, weak and strong. We must accept and understand these qualities within ourselves and hear and understand them in the opposite sex as well.

In fact, even though a man may not understand everything his wife is feeling, he can still cheer her on as she finds her inner voice, and he can help create an environment where she feels the freedom and safety to do so. In turn, a woman who knows herself and speaks her true voice will be a better partner to him. She will be able to more clearly state what she thinks and what she needs, and she will be able to offer him help to be a better husband and mate. She will understand the important secret of finding her voice and using it.

Now What?

If you lose your voice, you will dis-member a part of yourself. You may have forgotten how to use your inner voice, perhaps long ago in some distant place in your past. Your challenge now is to re-member. To do that, you will need to embark on a journey, an expedition into your heart. What might you need on this journey?

First, you will need a healthy sense of adventure. This journey will take you to places you have not visited in a while, so bring along your sense of curiosity.

Second, you will need courage as you risk saying things you have not said in some time. You will practice thinking things and saying things that have been dormant in you for some time.

Third, you will need thoughtfulness as you integrate these renewed voices into who you are at this moment.

Integration may not come easy as you discover things about yourself that you may not have realized were there.

Finally, you will need compassion for yourself and others. Some people may not welcome your true voice, and it may be disconcerting to some. Your new voice may be frightening to those around you and to yourself.

Adventure, courage, thoughtfulness, compassion—these will help you in your quest for your own voice. Rich rewards await you along the way.

Ten

The True Source of Power

*Perhaps the best way to thank God for the
gift of living is to appreciate the present hour,
to sit quietly and hear your own breathing and
look out on the universe and be content.*

LIN YUTANG

I received a phone call recently from a woman whose
name I knew but whom I had never formally met. She asked
to meet her for lunch to discuss ideas for her nonprofit
agency. I had mixed feelings about taking my time to listen,
but she assured me that she had no intention of trying to pressure me into anything. She only asked that I take a few minutes to listen and, after hearing what she had to say, to
consider the possibility of becoming involved. Judy met me at
a coffee shop downtown. I was immediately surprised by her
plain attire and her unassuming nature. Yet in spite of her lack
of glamour, she carried herself with dignity. She did not
need the external props of beauty or dress to exude a rare and
winsome grace. I was certain she would not be delivering a
high-pressure sales pitch.

We greeted one another and talked briefly about
knowing each other by name yet never crossing paths until

now. She had a broad, contagious smile, rosy cheeks, and an air of soft-spoken confidence. She looked me straight in the eyes and made no apologies for the purpose of her requested lunch: She wanted to share her vision with me and, if I shared her dream, enroll me in the project.

After exchanging pleasantries, Judy began explaining her brainchild. She leaned forward on the table, making notes on her paper and pointing to them excitedly for me to see. She held her head high, spoke distinctly, and gave me a direct, commanding gaze. She spoke of her job as director of a shelter for grieving families of those dying from various illnesses. It was a nonprofit agency, and she was brainstorming ways of growing her venture. She had faith that this "child" of hers would grow because God had called it to grow. It was something beyond her own making. Indeed, it was not even hers. God had given her the responsibility of raising this child. Her task was simply to function as a midwife through its birth and growth. She did not sound anxious because she had no reason to. "I need to just stay out of the way," she said, "and let God do what God wants to do."

Staying out of the way and letting God do what God wants to do. This has been a revolutionary concept for me, one who prides himself in making things happen. Getting out of the way has never been one of my strong suits, yet I marveled at this woman's strength and majestic countenance. She had a vision, a clear voice, and a path that invigorated her. Failure was impossible because she understood she was simply a vehicle for the greater purpose of God.

And here is our final secret for transforming your life: *Discover the true source of power for change.* When we let God do the transforming work, all we have to do is get out of the way.

Putting the Pieces Together

The woman at the coffee shop attracted my attention because she was clearly unique. She seemed to be in sync with herself, not fighting her way through life as many of us seem to do. And she understood the secret of getting out of the way of her self, listening to God, and doing His will for her life. But oh how difficult this can be.

Despite the horrific results of running our own lives, the evidence of our misspent power, we cling tenaciously to our worn-out ways of behaving. And far too often, we become discouraged and disenchanted with life.

We have learned many new skills, confronted many lies, and unearthed new truths that can transform us. We have talked about small, seemingly innocuous lies that subtly alter the course of our lives, restricting our potential with unnecessary limitations. The lies may be debilitating, but our acceptance of those lies can cause the worst kind of depression. We adjust our lives according to what we believe. When you believe, for example, that minor changes are good enough, you settle for so little in your life. When you believe all the excuses to stay the same in areas that desperately need changing, you settle again for your old life, the one you wanted so badly to transform. When you believe that everything is your fault instead of letting each person take responsibility for his or her part in the destruction, change cannot occur. When you shrink back from trusting and using your voice, change cannot happen. Positive, dynamic change can occur only when your powerful, incisive voice combines with the power of God to remake your life.

Most importantly, you have learned that each and every lie must be deliberately challenged. Your life may be like a quilt that has the wrong pieces in the wrong places. As you examine what you hoped would be a masterwork, you notice the errors. You may be discouraged at first because you realize that you have hours of reparative work ahead. But you see the task that must be undertaken. You must sit down, study the quilt and its stitching, and painstakingly undo some of your work. The right pieces must be put in the right places. Anything short of that may give you a quilt, but it will not be the masterpiece you are after. It will not be the work of art that you are capable of creating. You know you are capable of something better. Now is the time to stop delaying. The only solution is to jump in and begin your work.

Self-Will Run Riot

By now, you may feel empowered to change your ordinary life into something extraordinary. However, you may still feel a little shaky on your feet. Taking new truths and applying them to our lives is no easy matter. The skills and truths are many and varied, and we have practiced doing things in certain ways in spite of less than satisfying results. We spend an incredible amount of energy protecting our precious self.

Those in the Alcoholics Anonymous 12-step programs will readily recognize the concept of self-will. Simply put, it is the notion that left to our own crafty devices, we can self-destruct in a nanosecond. The wily self, bent on its own ways, will most often lead us down a treacherous path to a canyon of despair. Who has not fallen into this ravine of self-direction, only to emerge, bruised and battered, ready to attempt the same dangerous path again? Who has not succumbed to the immature posturing of the ego, only to look back and see the havoc it creates? This is self-will run riot. But now we know the truth that can set us free: God, the true source of power, can enliven us, change us, and give our lives true direction.

The 12-step program invites us to turn our lives over to God and find nourishment for our souls in Him. Under our own steam we are left sputtering, gasping for breath, wondering how in the world we will find the strength to climb the next mountain, ford the next stream, and make our way to the promised land. We can achieve this only by giving our lives over to God. We must live close to our spiritual nature and let go of our egomaniacal strivings.

Letting Go

Perhaps the biggest challenge facing us as we consider embracing God, the true source of power for change, is displacing the almighty ego from the throne of our lives. The EGO—Easing God Out—does not want to give up its hold on us. A coup is often necessary to overthrow this tyrant.

Perhaps you have not thought of the ego in this way. Perhaps you have learned to love, honor, and protect the precious self. Perhaps you have not considered that this aspect of our nature almost always reaches beyond its healthy bounds. If we are weak, the ego is more than happy to step in and run the show. We must assert ourselves and let our spiritual nature be the louder voice. Perhaps others have encouraged you to promote your inner willpower, telling you that you have all the strength you will ever need to march strongly forward, even in the face of the greatest adversity. This is common New Age advice, and you can easily fall victim to its enchantment. After all, your ego loves to hear people tell you that you have all the answers inside and that you need not listen to any other voices. But I suggest you reconsider.

I ask you to consider that the best way back from the chasm of confusion is to let go. But what in the world does "letting go" mean? Sound advice comes to us from Melody Beattie, an author who popularized the notion of letting go.

> We surrender to God's will. We stop trying to control and we settle for a life that is manageable....We're learning, through trial and error, to separate our will from God's will. We're learning that God's will is not offensive.[1]

According to Beattie, "letting go" means listening in a deeper way to what God is saying. It means cultivating a relationship with God so that you can discern His voice and separate it from the voice of the ego that clamors for increasing power. It means seeing, in new and fresh ways, that our own strivings for control, money, prestige, and other accoutrements will never satisfy the soul.

The Calculating Self

Watching someone use their personal power, their "calculating self," to get their way can be embarrassing. It is embarrassing because we can see ourselves in their manipulations. We watch as people jockey around like race car drivers at Indianapolis, trying to force their way past others.

This calculating self is the part of our ego that wants its own way regardless of the cost. Enter any classroom of first graders and you will see all kinds of posturing to see who can get first spot in the lunch line, sit closest to the teacher, or show off the biggest and best of whatever is popular at the moment. The calculating ego is alive and well in this microcosm of the larger world. We train the calculating self at an early age, and it gains momentum and tenacity in adult life.

Advance a few years, and you will see the same posturing taking place in the work world. Enter the boardroom of a major corporation and notice the similar maneuvering for personal advantage. Children, now in adult bodies, compete for the head seat at the table. Verbal jousting, mental gymnastics, gesturing, and even body posturing and positioning are used to climb over others to reach the top of the corporate ladder.

A wonderful illustration of the calculating self is found in Benjamin and Rosamund Zanders' fine book, *The Art of Possibility:*

> Two prime ministers are sitting in a room discussing affairs of state. Suddenly a man bursts in, apoplectic with fury, shouting and stamping and banging his fist on the desk. The resident prime

minister admonishes him: "Peter," he says "kindly remember Rule Number Six," whereupon Peter is instantly restored to complete calm, apologizes, and withdraws. The politicians return to their conversation, only to be interrupted yet again 20 minutes later by a hysterical woman gesticulating wildly, her hair flying. Again, the intruder is greeted with the words: "Marie, please remember Rule Number Six." Complete calm descends once more, and she too withdraws with a bow and an apology. When the scene is repeated a third time, the visiting prime minister addresses his colleague: "My dear friend, I've seen many things in my life, but never anything as remarkable as this. Would you be willing to share with me the secret of Rule Number Six?" "Very simple," replies the resident prime minister. "Rule Number Six is Don't take yourself so seriously." "Ah," says his visitor, "that is a fine rule." After a moment of pondering, he inquires, "And what, may I ask, are the other rules?" "There aren't any."[2]

Because the ego takes itself so seriously and believes that it can solve all of its own problems, it fails to acknowledge the need for any authority higher than itself. The calculating self has its origins in the garden of Eden, where Adam and Eve decided that they knew what was best and aspired to know more. In the end, they set out to be more and do more than their true nature was capable of. With the help of Satan, they conspired to solve their own problems. That same conspiratorial nature is alive and well in us today. Inevitably, it gets us into trouble at every turn in our lives.

The Zanders go on to discuss this calculating self by suggesting that the ego sees the world as one of...

- scarcity
- competition
- attention-seeking
- manipulation
- childishness

Lest we be too critical of this calculating self, the Zanders remind us what psychologists have long known: The ego's manipulative strategies are all designed to protect the anxious child from feelings of abandonment and loss. Because none of us are comfortable in this "one down" position of the immature ego, we develop personality traits that make us feel more powerful and at ease with ourselves.

But what is the impact of these traits on interpersonal relationships? How do these immature qualities play out in our marriages? In a word, they create havoc. Relying on the ego only exacerbates our condition. Acting out of scarcity leaves us striving for more and more, being competitive creates division, seeking attention isolates us from others, manipulating causes resentment, childishness creates disdain and scorn.

Clearly, these traits do not serve us well in the long run although they may bring us a short-term sense of accomplishment and control. Whether we are dealing with our colleagues at work or our partner in marriage, the calculating self only complicates our efforts to create love and respect with others.

The Central Self

The Zanders contrast the *calculating self*—and their perception of it as a worldview that life is about making progress, striving for success, and positioning oneself in the human hierarchy—with the *central self.* Here again they tell a story to illustrate the point.

> Inscribed on five pillars in the Holocaust Memorial at Quincy Market in Boston are stories that speak of the cruelty and suffering in the camps. The sixth pillar presents a tale of a different sort, about a girl named Ilse, a childhood friend of Guerda Weissman Kline, in Auschwitz. Guerda remembers that Ilse, who was about six years old at

the time, found one morning a single raspberry somewhere in the camp. Ilse carried it all day long in a protected place in her pocket, and in the evening, her eyes shining with happiness, she presented it to her friend Guerda on a leaf. "Imagine a world," writes Guerda, "in which your entire possession is one raspberry, and you give it to your friend."[3]

If the calculating self always looks out for Number One by protecting its interests, the central or spiritual self lets go and speaks and acts from a deeper place, a place connected to God that listens for the work of the Spirit in the world. If the calculating self is empowered by the shallow musings of the ego, the central self is empowered by the living, breathing power of God in our lives.

Imagine what would happen in your marriage if you were able, even for a short time, to set aside selfish interests and care for your partner in ways that would strengthen the bonds of love. Imagine your home when, even if your partner is immature and self-seeking, you call forth in him that deeper, more mature man. Imagine that instead of taking him on in battle, you were big enough to set aside the conflict and agree to a form of collaboration that seeks solutions from a spiritual perspective. Instead of a downward spiral, a lose-lose proposition, you would be able to envision a much larger world of win-win possibilities.

Healing Your Relationship with God

None of this sacrificial, spiritual collaboration with one another is possible, of course, without first establishing a connection to the spiritual source of power. Sadly, this is difficult for many couples because they have abandoned their vital relationship with the creative power of the universe. This broken connection must be repaired and the life source reestablished before God's healing work can take place in a marriage.

How do we begin to repair our relationship with God? If this is an area of your life that has been sorely lacking, moving from a world controlled by ego to one guided by the Spirit of God may seem next to impossible. In their bestselling book *Experiencing God*, Henry Blackaby and Claude King provide answers:

> God Himself pursues a love relationship with you. He is the One who takes the initiative to bring you into this kind of relationship. He created you for a love relationship to Himself. That is the very purpose of your life. This love relationship can and should be real and personal to you.[4]

Blackaby and King offer two key ingredients for establishing this essential bond. They note the importance of obedience and love as prerequisites for a loving relationship with God (John 14:15; Mark 12:30). Everything about knowing and experiencing God depends upon loving Him. They add, "When you do love God, He promises to respond with His blessings. You and your children will live under His blessings...He wants you to love Him with all your being."[5]

Loving God demands a dedicated relationship and commitment similar to those you share with your spouse and your children. It takes time and concerted effort. Relationships do not just happen incidentally. They require focus and intentionality. Thankfully, God never gives up on us and is always readily available for conversation.

You may be telling yourself that you have been hurt in your pursuit of God. But God is not responsible for the hurting. Friends, family, and church members may be misguided in their attempts to help you find God. In the process, perhaps by offering you myriad rules and regulations to live by, they may have hurt you. People are fallible. Their good intentions, sometimes gone awry, must never stop you from seeking God in an atmosphere of compassion that is still available in many churches today. We can always follow a path back to God if we choose to.

Laura's Story

Laura struggled for years in her marriage. Filled with the dissatisfaction of 20 years of a contentious relationship, she was ready to call it quits when she came to see me.

"There is nothing terribly wrong with my marriage. We just don't seem to be close to each other anymore. We make up after we quarrel, but each conflict seems to create greater distance between us. I'll admit that we act like spoiled children at times. He sulks and pouts; I withdraw into silence. We make up and then do it all over again. But we never solve anything. It's gotten to the point where I've lost hope that our marriage will ever amount to more than two people sharing a house together. Every time we fight, I lose respect for him and even for myself. I know this is not the way it's suppose to be."

She told me that she had read every self-help book on the market. I applauded her tenacity in trying to find solutions to her marital problem. Her marriage problems were many, but a deeper problem was her attempt to create change from a worldly perspective. She sought cosmetic changes, as so many people do, rather than deep change. She tried to rationalize the problems in her marriage and work them out with her husband. They tried to talk themselves into behaving differently, but at their core being nothing changed. I could hardly fault her commitment. However, her efforts lacked godly wisdom and power.

"You seem to be doing a lot of things right," I said. "You have listened to counsel from many sources, yet I wonder if you have sought out biblical counsel as well. How much time do you devote to praying about your marriage and seeking solutions using God-given strength?"

"I guess I don't really give much time to praying about our marriage. I think about what God would say and know that there are answers for me at church and in the Bible. But I admit that I don't take the time to study and pray like I should."

"That might be an important component to add to the list of things you are already trying. Maybe your husband will sit down with you and ask God to change your inner nature and his. I bet that if you commit yourselves to praying about specific character changes you would like to see, you will notice results."

Laura came to her appointment several weeks later quite excited. She had approached her husband about the prospect of reading the Bible and praying about some of the areas they seemed to fight about repeatedly. He wanted change as much as she and was willing to work on things from a biblical perspective. In the matter of a few short weeks, she already sensed that they might be able to break out of their entrenched behaviors and begin to heal their relationship.

David

While we know that David was a man after God's own heart, he was also a person with whom many of us can identify. For all of his godliness, he had a bundle of personal problems. He was jealous, materialistic, demanding, self-serving, a liar, and a murderer. Talk about a man who needed some counseling! David was a prime candidate.

Yet for all of his faults, we also know that this vulnerable, desperate man was willing to own his faults. He was willing to humble himself before God and man. He was willing to seek answers to his problems from the true source of power.

"I cry to the Lord; I call and call to him. Oh, that he would listen. I am in deep trouble and I need his help so much. All night long I pray, lifting my hands to heaven, pleading. There can be no joy for me until he acts" (Psalm 77:1-2 TLB).

This, of course, was not the only time David pleaded with God for help. God was the strength of his heart and mind. David wept and wailed for the Creator to come to his assistance during his times of discouragement. And we know that God did come to him and offer him protection and peace. God did not always rush in to save David, but He always offered peace. And that same power and peace is yours and mine if we will call upon Him for guidance.

What Makes Him Tick?

Sadly, when we talk about reaching out to God for strength, power, and peace, men struggle. Men seem to be more stubborn than women and reluctant to cry "uncle" and give up their childish ways of dealing with problems. Men are often content to hang on to outdated ways of behaving in spite of the horrible repercussions on relationships. Admitting their shortcomings and humbling themselves before God is especially difficult.

As I write this, many men are experiencing a spiritual renewal. Promise Keepers and other men's movements across the nation are reaching thousands of men. Many have met to grieve the loss of their fathers and, more importantly, their lost connection to themselves and God. I would like to think that more men are pondering these losses and are seeking to heal their broken relationships. I would like to think that the changes they found at some of these conferences have had a lasting impact. Unfortunately, based on what I witness on a daily basis, I am not convinced this is true.

What can women do in response to this lack of godly connection in the lives of their men? Must women remain the spiritual leaders in the homes because their husbands have abdicated that responsibility? These questions have no easy answers. However, I can offer a few observations.

First, a woman must be responsible for her own relationship with God. She cannot coerce or cajole her husband into going to church, praying, or becoming a godly leader in his home. She must keep her own spiritual fires strong and vibrant.

Second, a woman can be an example to her husband and children by keeping her relationship with God fresh and alive. She can be sure that her husband and children will be watching for the fruit that comes from nurturing her relationship with God.

Finally, she can trust God to supply her with the answers she will need to make good decisions that involve her welfare and those of their children. God is faithful to offer wisdom to those who seek it.

Now What?

The time has come for you to apply the secrets in this book and the wisdom of the Scriptures to your life. It is time to put some leather to your walk and take stock of the changes that must occur.

We have explored the importance of discovering the true source of power. Our source of power is the wisdom that comes from a dynamic, living relationship with God. Make Him the strength of your life, and you will find answers to the problems you face, including those that damage your relationship with your mate. As you are grounded in the Word of God and develop a dynamic spiritual life, you will know the right course of action and will feel at peace with it.

Change in your relationship will not come easily. The path to transformation has no shortcuts—even for Christians. As you occasionally review the secrets in this book, ask God to give you the courage to apply each one to your life. Do that, and a wonderful marriage awaits you.

"Seek first his kingdom and his righteousness, and all these things will be given to you as well" (Matthew 6:33).

Eleven

Maintaining Your Momentum

*One of the pleasantest things
in the world is the journey.*

WILLIAM HAZLITT

In his prize-winning book *The Alchemist*, Paulo Coelho tells the story of Santiago, a restless young boy who was coming of age and anxious to see the world. His father discouraged travel as a waste of time and money, yet he secretly admired his son's courage and sense of adventure. He told Santiago that all he could ever want was available in his own country. But his father could feel the pulse of desire within Santiago and, having lost his own opportunity to seek fortune, blessed the boy with three gold coins to buy a flock of sheep that would sustain him on his quest to see the world. The monies he earned from his trade would provide him the means to continue his nomadic life. Santiago sensed that his father's unspoken encouragement revealed a secret dream that Santiago would live out in his own travels.

And so Santiago, with his herd of sheep, went from town to town in the remote regions of Spain seeking adventure. For some time, the simple enjoyment of travel kept him going. He visited new castles, new people, and new lands. Much of his energy, however, was spent on keeping his sheep healthy so that he could eventually revisit his customers and sell them his wool. Perhaps his life was not much different than that of the psalmist David as he tended his sheep and kept them from danger.

As is the case with most adventures, Santiago's journey soon began taking interesting twists and turns. The journey itself, rather than any particular destination, became his chief prize.

One day a storekeeper's daughter caught his eye, and travel alone lost some of its magical spell on Santiago. But he was shy and insecure and did not pursue her. Once he was on his way again, he realized that he would not pass through her town again for an entire year. Would she remember him? Would she still hold the same charm he remembered? These questions kept him awake at night as the months passed and his journey brought him closer to her town.

As he lay down to sleep one evening, he wrestled with his feelings. He vainly attempted to remain cool in his affections toward her. Surely, he had no chance to win her. What if another shepherd with a larger herd than his had already come by and asked for her hand? But then he reminded himself of something we all think about. "It's the possibility of having a dream come true that makes life interesting."[1]

Journeys

Literature and life are filled with the journey. Reading *Gulliver's Travels* evokes a plethora of images. Ernest Hemingway takes us to different places with tension-filled adventures. *A Farewell to Arms* transports us into the Italian army and lets us live for a moment enmeshed in another culture. Who can forget the quirky encounters of Sancho Panza and Don Quixote? Here we see our lead character charge windmills as if they were the enemy. Don Quixote's self-image produces an error in perception that leads to all kinds of unusual adventures. The message seems to be clear: Even the sanest people at times have mistaken perceptions that lead them into trouble.

Many of us have been introduced to writers who lead us on an inward journey of the soul. Writers such as Henry David Thoreau cause us to see the world from another perspective. Who can read *Walden* and not walk away with a new, intimate perspective of life? And truly seeing, we are able to appreciate life and its beauty on a deeper level. The list could go on and on. We are all in the midst of a journey of one sort or another, whether external, internal, or both.

Traveling from one place in our lives to another, we cling tenaciously to the dream that we are always moving to higher and firmer ground where love and romance await. We hope that we are nearing that place where we are engaged in a wonderful, loving relationship that will make our heart skip a beat. I trust that you have caught a glimpse of that hope as you have traveled with me through the nine secrets of this book. I trust that you are anxious to try each and every secret and take delight in the results it brings.

But a journey is, among other things, a dynamic process. You never fully arrive. We are excited to get to where we are heading and perhaps frightened that we may never make it. The traveling is easier if we follow several principles discussed in this final chapter.

You have now read and interacted with nine secrets that are yours for the taking. You can use each liberally to create a better love relationship with your spouse. And they work. In this final chapter, I offer a few additional principles to enhance the nine secrets. If you add these three concepts to the nine secrets you have already learned, you will experience even greater success.

Maintaining Your Focus

They had probably been fishermen for generations. They, like their fathers and their fathers' fathers, had learned the trade of fishing. They knew it like the backs of their hands. It was not merely the way they made their financial living, it was their entire way of life. The disciples were a rugged bunch, and many of them had practiced their trade since they were young. It was what they focused upon each and every day because it was a part of their most essential identity.

Imagine their surprise, and perhaps fear, when Jesus challenged them. "'Come, follow me,' Jesus said, 'and I will make you fishers of men'" (Matthew 4:19). What could this man possibly mean? Fishing for men? Ridiculous. This language sounded quixotic at best. Yet He challenged them to give up their way of living and embrace a new focus.

Perhaps some of the secrets found in this book have seemed as absurd and out of reach to you. *What? Try this new method of doing things when I have been doing things my own way for years? I can't do that.*

Yes, you can. And if you want to really learn some new tools for improving your marriage, you must not only try these new methods of communication and behaving but you must maintain your focus. You can easily become sidetracked with daily distractions and lose your focus. But the advice I have given you isn't a quick fix that you can discard at dusk.

I remember reading about the "tyranny of the urgent" some time ago. The concept had to do with all the little challenges that call for our attention on a daily basis. We try multitasking as if this were a natural and healthy way to live. But as we tackle every urgent thing that comes along, we often forget to take care of the truly important matters in our lives. Driven to distraction, we no longer focus on the real priorities in our lives and especially in our relationships.

Rocky

A young man with youthful vigor and stamina decides to go against all odds and take on a potentially unbeatable adversary. Many of us enjoy this kind of plot. An over-matched, everyday man goes up against the larger opponent for a chance to win it all. But to do so will take every ounce of energy, riveted focus, and dogged determination.

Who can forget the scenes where Rocky Balboa decides to take on his nemesis, Apollo Creed? The unlikely story pits a small-time boxer against the heavyweight champ. The underdog's goal is to go the distance, and the prize is his self-respect. The story unfolds with many memorable scenes. Rocky trains mercilessly while the orchestral score draws in the audience. He is focused. He has one thing and one thing only on his mind: victory, regardless of the price.

This unlikely story has Hollywood written all over it, yet people flooded the theaters to see the smaller, weaker, less capable man take on his infinitely more talented foe. We love to see the spoils go to the man with the bigger heart. We can identify with an underdog. Perhaps we too feel like we are taking on the entire world without any great equalizer.

But let's look deeper at how this may apply to us. What Rocky lacks in brains and experience, he makes up for with heart and focus. He develops a training regimen that would put the Green Berets to shame. He eats, sleeps, and drinks victory. He understands the price of winning and is willing to punish his body and his mind to get there. In the process he earns our admiration and, surprisingly, pulls himself up to a place where he has a chance of winning.

The Marathon

Not long ago, a friend of mine challenged me to run the Portland Marathon with him. "A marathon!" I said incredulously. "That's 26.2 miles!"

"Come on," he chided me. "We can train together."

"I'll think about it," I said, trying to humor him.

I had no desire to run 26.2 miles in a week, let alone a day. But his offer intrigued me, and I wondered if I really could be one of Those People Who Run Marathons. Could I really endure the training required to run the entire course without passing out, getting sick, or having to be carted off to a hospital in a sag wagon? I decided to talk to him more about his absurd offer.

"Can a person really train enough to run a marathon without passing out halfway through?" I asked.

"Yes," he replied, "but it will take focus. You will have to train for several months. We will have to run almost every day and increase our mileage each week. If we follow my training plan, we can finish the marathon."

"Okay," I said somewhat reluctantly. "Let's do it."

During the next two months, my friend and I trained. And trained. And trained. I watched *Rocky* a time or two, replaying the theme song in my mind like an anthem that pushed me to stick with the painful training regimen. We talked almost exclusively about the training plan and how we were feeling. Some days went smoothly. Other days were incredibly difficult. Sometimes I was out of town on business yet had to find the hours and energy to go out and run several miles. Once I was traveling in Norway and had to leave my friends and run for three hours in a foreign city! My training was exacting a lot from me. But I wanted to run this marathon and finish it to prove something to myself. The prize would be worth the pain. And so I maintained my focus.

As the time for the marathon neared, I felt strong. I could cover 18 miles without becoming exhausted. The training manual that promised a strong finish with the right preparation appeared to be right. I was focused, tuned up, and set to go.

The day of the race arrived, and we were ready. With water bottles and power bars attached to our hip packs, we set out with thousands of others to travel what had initially seemed like an impossible distance. But preparation and focus had equipped us to go the distance with a little extra juice in our tanks to boot. I was surprised and elated as I crossed the finish line with my friend.

Starting any race is easy. Picking up this book and reading it has been a good beginning for you. The fact that you have read this book shows that you are interested in running the race. You have read and considered each secret. Perhaps you have even begun applying them to your marriage. But I must caution you. Starting is not enough. Maintaining your focus is a critical element in the process. You must stay the course. In spite of the obstacles that you will undoubtedly face, you must keep plugging along until you reach the goal that you have set.

The apostle Paul understood the concept of focus. Listen to his words:

> Do you not know that in a race all the runners run, but only one gets the prize? Run in such a way as to get the prize. Everyone who competes in the games goes into strict training. They do it to get a crown that will not last; but we do it to get a crown that will last forever. Therefore, I do not run like a man running aimlessly; I do not fight like a man beating the air. No, I beat my body and make it my slave so that after I have preached to others, I myself will not be disqualified for the prize (1 Corinthians 9:24-27).

Debbie's Journey

Debbie, a 32-year-old wife and mother of two young sons, came to see me after she had become embittered about her marriage. Her life had become an emotional roller coaster. She was haggard, had bags under her eyes, and voiced bitterness and anger repeatedly.

Debbie was drifting toward hopelessness and desperately needed change in her marriage. Even visits to her pastor, together with her husband, had failed to bring about the changes she so badly desired in her marriage. She wanted more attention and consideration from her workaholic husband, and she had come to realize that she had nagged him to change for too long. She had used too many words and not nearly enough action. She had minimized the severity of the problem, making excuses for his busyness. But even with these insights, taking action and maintaining a focus did not come easily.

Initially discouraged and ready to give up on her marriage, she read some of the information in this book and became excited about applying its secrets. She felt "armed and ready for action." However, as is the case with many of the dreams we desire and pursue, she failed to calculate the distance of the race. Initially energized and enthusiastic about possible changes in her marriage, she lost her focus along the way. She became distracted and then was disillusioned when the change process did not play out as smoothly and effortlessly as she had hoped.

Our counseling sessions became something like a football huddle. I helped Debbie regain her focus and encouraged her to maintain her plan of action. I helped her to see that her discouragement came from losing focus and leaving the game plan. It was not a sign that change was impossible in her marriage.

Progress was slow at the start, and we had to battle against disappointment and near-depression. She had falsely thought that the secrets would quickly and easily translate into a new life and that her husband would do handstands to change for her. The cheering section she imagined would be there for her evaporated. And when it did, she felt alone and weak.

"I didn't think it would be this hard," Debbie said. "Somehow I thought that I would just try these new techniques, Glen would change, and that would be that. I didn't plan on him resisting, and I didn't realize how easy it would be for me to become distracted. I forgot that I still have diapers to change, a job to go to, and a class to teach at church. All of these things keep going on while I am trying to practice this new way of behaving. I need to keep encouraging myself to stay focused on using these new tools."

During her counseling sessions, I reminded her to stay focused and keep following her plan of action. As she did so, she noticed positive changes. Glen began to take her more seriously. He gradually began to understand the severity of the problems in their marriage. These positive changes built upon themselves, and she was able to regain the momentum that she had temporarily lost.

Sadly, people commonly become discouraged and lose heart. We forget that things naturally regress. In fact, the principle of *entropy* states that all things are in a natural state of decay. We will all tend to fall off course. Maintaining our focus takes rigorous effort. We need not become disillusioned when we forget our original goals or become inconsistent. Rather, we have only to steer ourselves back on course and stay focused as best we can. In nearly all cases, this will be good enough to bring about change.

Maintaining Your Purpose

In the middle of a hot, humid day, Jesus walked along a dusty road in Samaria, thirsty from the parching sun. He purposely traveled through this region though its residents did not welcome Jews. These people had little to do with one another, and most Jews simply bypassed this area to avoid the disdain of the Samaritans. Yet Jesus didn't follow customary protocol. We read in John's Gospel that Jesus did the unthinkable, asking a Samaritan woman for a drink of water. We read that the woman "was surprised that a Jew would ask a 'despised Samaritan' for anything" (John 4:9 TLB). Not only does He ask for a drink, but He also proceeds to talk to her about life. He does not judge or condemn her; He offers her kindness and compassion.

The disciples are understandably perplexed. Jesus had defied tradition. He spoke to a woman. He spoke to a Samaritan woman. He asked her for a drink. He carried on a long conversation with her, going against all societal norms and customs. Why? Because He had a larger purpose that His disciples failed to comprehend. The disciples were focused on the smaller picture. All they could see was that their leader was acting in an outrageous manner. They had a narrow view of how things ought to be. No doubt they wanted to take Jesus aside and set Him straight. Can you hear them saying, "Look, Jesus. What do you think You're doing? You shouldn't be talking to a Samaritan woman. We hate these people, and we don't want others to see us talking to them." But if they had stuck to their narrow point of view, they would have missed the bigger picture: Jesus' purpose for coming to earth.

Repeatedly Jesus instructs His disciples. Repeatedly He maintains His focus and His purpose. He never loses sight of why He is here and what He is trying to accomplish. Everything He does fits into a larger plan. He goes on to share with the disciples and with us that His purpose is to do the will of God, harvesting souls for the kingdom.

A reading of the Gospels gives the impression that the disciples consistently didn't get the message. They repeatedly lost sight of Jesus' purpose in coming to earth. In fact, one gets the impression that perhaps they never were fully able to see the big picture. We would do well not to be too critical of them, however, because we too often lose perspective. We forget why we are doing what we are doing, or worse, we forget what we have set out to do in the first place.

After you've read this book and examined its nine secrets, you may easily lose your focus and your purpose. Ask yourself why it is important to remain clear about your purpose in practicing these secrets. The answer will be very apparent. You want significant changes in your marriage. Now is the time to remind yourself that you will only get them if you remain focused and clear about your purpose.

A New Mission Statement

Many companies today have found value in creating a "mission statement." This mission statement usually contains a company's purpose, a concise explanation of why they are in existence. In that incisive, clear statement, they have articulated the reason they have come together. Perhaps a company's mission is to deliver the best pizza in town in the least amount of time. Perhaps it is to offer excellent insurance at affordable rates. Perhaps it is to provide clean rooms and friendly hospitality to each and every person who comes to them. Whatever the mission statement, it is designed to keep the organization focused and on course. Written in bold letters in their company policy manual, it is a constant reminder of why they have come together to form a business.

Perhaps you have heard about the world famous fish marketers of Pike Place Fish Market in Seattle, Washington. They have taken this notion of purpose to a new level. A group of folks up in that rainy neck of the woods set out to make their fish company the best that it could be. They decided to make tossing fish to their customers a work of art, a place of fun, and a source of entertainment to those passing by. They reflected upon their chosen purpose, their reason to be in business, and what they wanted their customers to think about them. They created a mission statement that is outlined in the popular book *Fish,* by Stephen Lundin, Harry Paul, and John Christensen. In this book they share how they took a mediocre and relatively obscure fish company and made it world famous. They accomplished this by utilizing four principles:

- Choose: Make today a great day.
- Play: Be very serious about your work without taking yourself too seriously at work.
- Be There: Don't let distractions destroy the quality that is present in each moment.

- Make Their Day: Find someone who needs a helping hand, a word of support, or a good ear.[2]

The mission statement came about because the management of the Pike Place Fish Market decided to take the company to a new level. In the same way, you want to take your marriage to a new level. That won't just happen. It will happen only if you remain deliberate about what you are doing. It will happen only by maintaining your focus, your purpose, and your momentum.

Many individuals and families have applied a similar tool in their own lives. They have discovered that thinking through a mission statement for life helps to guide them to where they want to go. It becomes a roadmap for guiding them on their journey.

Stop, look, and listen. Remind yourself why you believe things need to change. What is wrong with your relationship that needs adjustment? What have you learned about yourself that you now want to change? What do you want to do differently? And, most importantly, What is your purpose for changing? Write out your purpose, much like a mission statement, so that you can always be clear about what you are reaching for.

As I worked with Debbie, I asked her to consider how she had come to be in this situation. As I have done for you in this book, I emphasized to her that every difficulty is an opportunity to grow. While she was tempted to reiterate how Jim was victimizing her, I encouraged her to take control of her life and consider what she could learn from this challenge. I asked her to place her struggles in the context of a mission statement. I asked her to write out her purpose for changing. She initially resisted this exercise but eventually accepted it. The final product looked like this:

> I am practicing these nine secrets because I want more intimacy in my marriage. I want to stop minimizing my problems and expecting them to

disappear. I want to get more love and affection from my husband, and communicating with him clearly about this will help me get the things I need. I want to stay focused on positive change and, using godly wisdom, continue to apply all my efforts to create intimacy with my husband. I will stop at nothing short of that.

Debbie's statement of purpose was a dynamic tool that she used for positive change. She revised it periodically to emphasize what particular tool she might be working on at that time. She also encouraged her husband to outline his purpose for change and the tools he would use to achieve it. This turned out to be a very powerful strategy for their marriage.

The Heart of the Matter

Many people who are interested in change look upon their problems in a very superficial way. They simply want relief, not inner heart change. But as you have learned, superficial change does not last. Soon the problem reappears, and we act surprised.

Maintaining your purpose must include a change of heart. When we look at our problems through the eyes of the heart, change comes more easily. We may see the problem differently. We may realize that we are part of the problem. So beware. When you open your heart to the matter, things may change in an unexpected way.

Stephen R. Covey understood these principles, and much of his bestselling book *The Seven Habits of Highly Effective People* focused on matters of the heart and living with purpose. His second habit, Begin with the end in mind, encourages readers to tap into those values they hold most deeply. Understanding and acknowledging these will help you maintain your mission and momentum.

To begin with the end in mind, Covey gives us the following instruction:

> Begin today with the image, picture, or paradigm of the end of your life as the frame of reference or the criterion by which everything else is examined. Each part of your life—today's behavior, tomorrow's behavior—can be examined in the context of the whole, of what really matters most to you. By keeping that end clearly in mind, you can make certain that whatever you do on any particular day does not violate the criteria you have defined as supremely important, and that each day of your life contributes in a meaningful way to the vision you have of your life as a whole.[3]

Covey goes on to say that to begin with the end in mind means to start with a clear understanding of your destination. This may sound ridiculously simple, but it is not. Many people get sidetracked because they are not clear about their goals and what they really want to accomplish. Covey strongly believes that real progress is made when we know where we are going and are aware of where we are now on that path. And he asserts,

> How different our lives are when we really know what is deeply important to us, and, keeping that picture in mind, we manage ourselves each day to be and to do what matters most. If the ladder is not leaning against the right wall, every step we take just gets us to the wrong place faster. We may be very busy, we may be very efficient, but we will also be truly effective only when we begin with the end in mind.[4]

Covey strongly believes in writing a personal mission statement, much like the one I helped Debbie write. He believes that a personal mission statement will reflect what you want to be (character) as well as what you want to do (contributions and achievements). When based on correct principles, a mission statement becomes a standard. It becomes a basis for making life-changing decisions in the midst of distracting circumstances and emotions. It provides a changeless core that keeps everything in perspective when life swirls about you. It allows you to flow with changes rather than become rattled by them.

Covey cites the mission statement of a woman who was seeking balance in her life and work:

> I will seek to balance career and family as best I can since both are important to me.
>
> My home will be a place where I and my family, friends, and guests find joy, comfort, peace, and happiness. Still I will seek to create a clean and orderly environment, yet livable and comfortable. I will exercise wisdom in what we choose to eat, read, see, and do at home. I especially want to teach my children to love, to learn, and to laugh—and to work and develop their unique talents....
>
> I will be a self-starting individual who exercises initiative in accomplishing my life's goals. I will act on situations and opportunities, rather than be acted upon.[5]

We can see in this example, as in Debbie's, that a personal mission statement can empower people to clarify what is truly important, to identify what is at the heart of the matter, and to assert how they can stay on course to accomplish their goals.

Jackie's Journey

Jackie was nearing the end of a six-month stint in counseling, pleased with her progress and thankful for the experience. She first came because she was unhappy in her marriage, but this 27-year-old woman now felt empowered and encouraged by the progress she had made and the changes she saw in her husband.

Jackie came to counseling with typical complaints. Her husband was critical, and she felt devalued. Having come from a family where her mother was also critical and her father absent, her husband's insensitivities found a vulnerable target.

Jackie had reminded her husband "hundreds of times" how much his biting sarcasm hurt her. Yet he persisted, explaining that he was only joking. His words did not seem funny to her, however, and in fact were quite hurtful.

When we explored how she tended to handle his destructive comments, she realized she had made many mistakes common to so many women. She had tried to ignore the problem, minimize the problem, and make excuses for the problem, but she had never fully addressed it. Using the secrets found in this book, she became empowered to make substantial improvements.

But as is also common to those beginning to make changes in their relationships, she was easily distracted from her goals. She would make progress, only to relapse into old behavior patterns. She would ride the roller coaster of change-encouragement-relapse-discouragement. She had a hard time keeping herself fixed firmly upon the goal.

Together Jackie and I explored the principles found in this chapter—ways to maintain her focus, purpose, and momentum. She wrote a personal mission statement, declaring why she was so committed to change. She found her desire for transformation was rooted deeply in one basic truth: She wanted a marriage filled with honor, integrity, and devotion. She did not want a relationship where sarcasm, criticism, and devaluing comments were commonplace.

When Jackie gained command of these principles, she asked her husband to join us. He was a bit embarrassed at first, but he soon came to see the value in the changes that had taken place in his wife. He was delighted in her newfound self-esteem and also liked the changes that he eventually came to make as well. Together they forged a new vision for their marriage based on sound biblical principles of love and sacrificial caring for one another. They now understand the importance of maintaining vigilance over their relationship and guarding against the backsliding that can happen so easily.

Maintaining Your Momentum

The game was tied at 64 as the final quarter started. The Bruins had led for much of the way while the Thunderbirds struggled to find their groove. The Bruins had led by 15 points late in the third quarter. A sudden surge by the Thunderbirds brought them to within three points near the end of the period, and just as the buzzer sounded, their star point guard nailed a three-pointer. Both teams knew that the momentum had shifted, and the team that had been behind all evening was now in good position to win the game.

Shifting momentum is a phenomenon clearly recognized by everyone in the world of sports. It is a palpable force that every athlete understands and respects. At this stage in the game, the Bruins would be well-advised to pull themselves together, review what is going wrong, and do what they can to summon their resources to shift the momentum back in their direction. If they fail to do so, the game will be in jeopardy.

Momentum occurs in the arena of human dynamics as well. As you have read this book and applied its secrets to your life, you may have felt a shift in momentum. You have experienced the pride of accomplishment, the joy of inner personal growth, the pleasure of increased intimacy with your spouse. You have acknowledged that God is truly a powerful force in your life who can bring about miraculous change. Hopefully, you have stopped and expressed thanks to Him for the revelations and changes He has blessed you with.

But now you want to continue the momentum into the weeks and months to come. You want to continue to grow and expand the areas of intimacy in your marriage. You do not want entropy to set in, erasing all that you have worked hard to achieve. As I have said, success in this area will require focus, a clear purpose, and momentum. But what will keep things going in a positive direction?

First, acknowledge the growth that you have made. You must sit back and review where you have been and what changes you have made. Look back over the past several months and reflect upon the positive growth that has taken place. Most importantly, determine what steps you have taken to cause change to occur.

Second, be thankful to God for allowing positive growth to take place. God is ultimately the author of all that is good, so He deserves ultimate credit for the changes. Stop and thank Him for the changes, both large and small.

People often fail to notice and thank God for the improvements that occur. Many little miracles pass by daily without any acknowledgement from us that God is alive and active in our lives. Open your eyes. Catch God doing wonderful things for you.

Third, ride the wave of success. Determine where the wave is taking you and project success out into the future. Watch for the open doors and be prepared to walk through them. Conversely, watch for the closed doors and don't try to simply barrel your way through. Use your God-given intuition to sense where your path is leading and follow it.

Finally, anticipate what still needs to change in the future. Look ahead and note those areas that still need attention. Where are the opportunities and challenges for growth? What issues in your marriage still need to be addressed? Outline them and hold them up for prayer.

Adopting Habits

Riding the wave of momentum includes creating positive habits. This is the process of linking one positive behavior to another until a habit is formed. Sometimes these are rather haphazard efforts that only come close to the end goal without achieving it, but they are positive steps, nonetheless. Psychologists call this process "successive approximation."

The process of change includes a series of behaviors that are often feeble attempts at reaching the ultimate goal. Too often, couples make the drastic error of insulting one another when these attempts fall short. Let me illustrate.

Robert and Rebecca were struggling to make changes they both wanted in their relationship. Sadly, many years of resentment had built serious obstacles. For example, when Robert committed to helping out around the house—something Rebecca had wanted for a long time—she was only slightly encouraged. She muttered in the counseling session, "I'll believe it when I see it." Her response brought an onslaught of negativity from Robert.

"You see what I'm up against?" he said. "I'll never be able to please her. The second I don't fold a towel right, she'll be down my neck."

"What do you expect?" she countered. "Am I supposed to praise you for doing something you should have been doing all along?"

Both had valid points. The real question was, how could they adopt new habits under these ominous conditions? The answer is that change happens slowly, in haphazard steps. Ideally, Robert will begin to make changes, Rebecca will notice and affirm him, and a shift in behavior will occur. Gradually the new behaviors become second nature and both partners feel affirmed, supported, and encouraged.

The danger is that an atmosphere of criticism may become pervasive, and neither partner will feel compelled to change. In fact, both will be tempted to act passive-aggressively toward one another. If they aren't careful, they will create an unhealthy distance, and the relationship will disintegrate.

When I counsel couples like Robert and Rebecca, I encourage them to create a positive environment where change is fostered. I help them see their responsibility to develop a climate where momentum can build.

The Life of Christ

Perhaps the best example of momentum is the life of Christ. Watching His life and ministry unfold, we see a man who was on a mission—a mission that gained momentum with each step He took along the way. A reading of the Gospels clearly shows us a man with a focus. Though He faced opposition, each piece eventually fit together like a jigsaw puzzle, revealing a picture of beauty.

As a youth He was interested in the things of God. He grew strong and robust and was filled with wisdom. He preferred to be in the temple, learning from the teachers of the law and "discussing deep questions." Family was important to Him, but His loved ones took a back seat to His ministry. He challenged them to understand that He was a man who knew His mission and purpose in life (Luke 2:40-50).

We know little about Jesus' development from His youth until His adulthood. Presumably, He continued to learn about the law and spent much of His time studying. He was undoubtedly focused. He knew that He would face challenges in the days ahead, and He prepared Himself for them. He knew that He would need a solid relationship with the Father to sustain Him during the days ahead. Toward that end, He spent many predawn hours in prayer with God. Here was a growing relationship!

The Gospels illustrate the unfolding of His ministry. We see the selection of a small group of followers, His disciples, and their instruction and training, preparing them to carry on His ministry after His departure. This method of promoting His ministry turned the world upside down.

As His ministry gathered momentum and His popularity increased, crowds gathered around Him. We read about Him healing many, performing miracles that astounded those who came from miles away to witness these events. Many saw and believed. Each day, new believers joined the growing ranks of converts.

However, Jesus didn't just gain momentum from the pressing crowds who sought Him to heal their infirmities. His momentum was aided by the distrust of the traditional religious community, which also grew. His challenges to the religious authorities ultimately led to a showdown. He seemed to take little caution in upsetting the Pharisees, whom He disdained. He made no bones about telling them they were hypocrites with little spiritual substance. A momentum of hostility was growing against Him.

As His life unfolded, everything occurred according to plan. The timing was, of course, perfect. Jesus needed time to develop His ministry, train His disciples, and teach and heal the people. Ultimately, His momentum carried Him to the day when He laid down His life. It was not taken from Him, as some have said. Rather, He knew the exact time that He was to sacrifice His life and the purpose for it. Everything occurred for a reason: to reveal to the world the need for a Savior.

Covenantal Momentum

Marriage is a union of two distinct people. Because people are so different, we are sometimes amazed that this institution works at all. But it does. It does because many couples ultimately succeed in fulfilling a covenantal vision. Let's consider what that may look like and how it may help us maintain momentum.

Much of this book has focused on making changes within yourself so that you are more likely to achieve behavioral changes in your spouse that will enhance your marriage. I believe that this is a valid and worthwhile goal as you critically examine your behavior in the context of your marriage. However, we dare not overlook the role of sacrificial love in marriage. Couples that are committed to creating changes that will enhance their relationship can gain momentum. After all, isn't that what love is all about?

Robert Morris, in his wonderful article "A Home for Love to Dwell: Covenant Relationship as Continual Conversion," says:

> Covenant relationships, in the Christian vision, are dedicated to the shaping of souls in which the domain of charity—active interest in the well-being of others—*grows steadily larger* [italics mine]. In the intimacy of small things—dachshunds, diapers, and dinners—our current habits are challenged in the name of a larger love. Ongoing relationships call us to embrace more and more of the other—and the part of the world to which the other opens us.[6]

Can you feel the relational momentum in this quote? As you begin making small behavioral changes with one another and grow in intimacy, your world will grow as well. The possibilities for an even deeper level of commitment will become available to you. A healthier marriage will be within your reach.

We close our time together with the understanding that we are all on a journey to know one another and to become known. And we realize that we cannot accomplish this unless God's love is resident within us. We need His help and wisdom to make these changes. As Robert Morris says, "So long as we are trapped in impatience, envy, boastfulness, arrogance, rudeness, irritability, or resentment, we are not free for this Love to move through us fully."[7] And we need His love to enter our lives and give us the courage to practice the secrets found in this book.

We need this love to be patient as our partner makes what may be feeble attempts at change and we practice accountability. We need this love to encourage us to continue to ride the wave of momentum we have started days or weeks before and to continue the journey.

Bless you as you continue the work that you have started by reading this book. Bless you as you maintain your focus, your purpose, and most of all, your momentum.

Believe that you can get what you want, and you will!

How to Help a Friend

Congratulations, again, on the hard work that you have done as you have worked through the nine secrets in this book. By now you have begun to apply them to your life and your marriage and are seeing some wonderful results. You have also practiced the art of maintaining your momentum and can see the danger of taking a step or two backward. Fortunately, you understand that growth does not always happen in a straight line but rather in a series of zigs and zags, always with new opportunities to practice the secrets.

Part of maintaining momentum includes living out the lessons you have learned. This often involves others in our lives, including our friends. As you became excited about the secrets in this book, you may have wanted to share them with a friend. This can be an excellent way for the secrets to come alive for you. By talking about them, practicing them, and encouraging your friends to live them out, you make them personal and alive for you.

Perhaps as you have worked through the chapters and the secrets, you have already discussed some of the concepts with your friends. Or perhaps you have thought about a friend who is going through similar struggles. You have wondered how you can be of help to them. You see them wrestle with the same issues, over and over again, and now wonder if you should, or can, do more to help. With this in mind I have put together a few ideas that will help you minister to your loved ones who struggle with a relationship that is not working. In addition to sharing the secrets of this book with them, consider the following tools and principles:

You cannot change anyone except yourself. Yes, you have heard these words before. I repeat them here because we are tempted to think of ourselves as omnipotent, able to lend a hand to anyone and rescue anyone from their deeply personal crisis. But we need a large dose of humility before we offer anyone counsel or support.

Don't get confused about how much power you actually have. Every person must, in the final analysis, take responsibility for his or her life alone. Do not feel responsible to rescue them or guilty for not being able to. Even if they appear caught in the quagmire of a bad marriage, you must remember your limitations.

Each person must take responsibility for his or her own life. Just as you must admit that you can change only your own life, the same is true for your friend. You may be tempted to see others as helpless, lost, or otherwise incapable of making different choices, but this is not true. They can, like you, make different choices that will alter their life for the better.

When we act as if they are capable of changing their life, we are in essence offering them a powerful gift. We are speaking to their strengths, noticing and commenting on their ability to act differently. We are reinforcing their unique talents and gifts, their wisdom to see and do things differently than they have done them in the past.

A small kindness can make a huge difference. Sometimes a little help from a friend can make a marvelous difference. You may feel as if you are doing nothing when you offer to listen and pray, but these can make all the difference in the world to a hurting friend. A little kindness here and a listening ear there can be lifesavers to someone hurting.

We often make the mistake of believing that we must offer profound wisdom or come up with the answer that will solve all of their problems. This is not the case and can actually be harmful. They do not need someone to rush in with all the answers, as if that were even possible. They need small acts of kindness more than anything.

Offer concrete help only when asked. As you consider offering them a book, such as this one, or specific advice, you must first make sure that they are asking for such help. Uninvited advice is not helpful, and people often resent it. Such unsolicited advice will create a barrier between you and them and may turn them off to future assistance.

Do you remember hurting and having someone walk up to you and tell you exactly what you need to do to solve all of your problems? These self-proclaimed prophets have an incredible need to rescue and an exaggerated sense of self-importance. Be careful of making the same mistake.

If asked, be utterly but tactfully truthful. I have often seen friends that will tiptoe around as if offering truthful feedback would kill them. Instead of possibly hurting feelings, they offer platitudes. "Of course you didn't do anything that could have led to you being rejected," we offer, knowing that is not the truth. And our friends know it.

So, offer truthful advice when it is solicited. Offer it carefully and lovingly, but offer it. You can offer it as a possibility for them to consider, not as a word given to you in a vision. Offer it as something that may have worked for you and that might work for them. But offer it.

Set healthy boundaries for yourself and them. You will do no good if you offer to always be available, anytime of the day or night. You have a life to live too, and if you don't take care of yourself, you will not be effective in caring for them. By managing your life effectively, you model behavior that will be helpful to them in the long run.

If they ask, tell them how you have set healthy boundaries for yourself in the past. Tell them how you continue to struggle with saying no or doing too much. Tell them what you are learning about boundaries and the powerful impact it is having on your life.

Be available, as you can, to help them pick up the pieces. Nothing is quite as wonderful as friends who are simply there, offering their presence. They are there to pick up the phone when it rings at odd hours. They are willing to put their own needs aside temporarily to help out. The consistency of the relationship is the healing factor. No magic words, no powerful elixirs. Just a calm presence that listens and seeks to understand.

Appendix 2

Self-Assessment

The following statements have been designed to help you assess your progress in applying the nine secrets to your personal life. Read each of the statements and answer it honestly. Score them as follows:

If you agree completely with the statement, score a 3. If you somewhat agree, score a 2. If you somewhat disagree with the statement, score a 1. If you completely disagree, score a 0.

1. I believe that I am utterly truthful with myself about my problems.

   0   1   2   3

2. I rarely make excuses about others' harmful behaviors.

   0   1   2   3

3. I rarely retreat into silence rather than seek support.

   0   1   2   3

4. I am ready and willing to make real changes in my life.

   0   1   2   3

5. I believe I can make changes to make my marriage better.

   0   1   2   3

6. I know that a little change is not enough to make things better.

   0   1   2   3

7. I am rarely afraid to take action that is needed in my marriage.

   0   1   2   3

8. I practice sharing my opinion with others.

   0   1   2   3

9. I have a good relationship with God and am strengthened by it.

   0   1   2   3

10. I maintain my focus, purpose, and momentum for positive change.

   0   1   2   3

Scoring: Add up your scores and analyze your responses.

20 and above: You appear to have made some very positive changes in your life and feel optimistic about future change.

15–20: You feel fairly optimistic about your life but know that some areas need additional improvement.

10–15: You are admitting that many areas need improvement. You may want to seek some additional support as you work on these areas.

Less than 10: You seem to be struggling with many of the secrets and may want professional help to work on these issues.

Notes

Chapter 1—The Lies We Believe

1. Les and Leslie Parrott, *Saving Your Marriage Before It Starts* (Grand Rapids, MI: Zondervan Publishing, 1995), 47.

2. Thomas Moore, *Care of the Soul* (New York: HarperCollins Publishers, 1998), 86.

3. Harriet Goldhor Lerner, *The Dance of Intimacy* (New York: Harper and Row, 1989), 208-09.

4. Don Miguel Ruiz, *The Four Agreements* (San Rafael, CA: Amber-Allen Publishing, 1997), 31-33.

5. Quoted in Robert Wicks, *Touching the Holy* (Notre Dame, IN: Ave Maria Press, 1992), 66.

Chapter 2—Be Truthful with Yourself

1. Paul Brand and Philip Yancey, *In His Image* (Grand Rapids, MI: Zondervan Publishing House, 1984), 23.

2. Patricia Evans, *Controlling People* (Avon, MA: Adams Media Corporation, 2002), 54.

Chapter 3—Stop Making Excuses

1. Quoted in Robert Wicks, *Touching the Holy* (Notre Dame, IN: Ave Maria Press, 1992), 124.

2. John Eldredge, *Wild at Heart* (Nashville, TN: Thomas Nelson Publishers, 2001), 45.

3. Mary Belenky, et al., *Women's Ways of Knowing* (New York: Basic Books, Inc., 1986), 29.

Chapter 4—The Inner Vow of Silence

1. Virginia Satir, *Peoplemaking* (Palo Alto, CA: Science and Behavior Books, 1972), 58.

2. John Bradshaw, *Healing the Shame That Binds You* (Deerfield Beach, FL: Health Communications, 1988), viii.

3. Ibid., 121.

Chapter 5—Real Change Requires Real Action

1. Rainer Maria Rilke, *Rilke on Love and Other Difficulties* (New York: W.W. Norton and Company, 1975), 30.

Chapter 6—It Can Be So Much Better

1. David Whyte, *Crossing the Unknown Sea* (New York: Riverhead Books, 2001), 6.

2. David Greibner, "Shadowbound," *Weavings* 6, no. 2 (March/April 1991), 32-33.

3. Lawrence Crabb, *The Marriage Builder* (Grand Rapids, MI: Zondervan Publishing Company, 1982), 20.

Chapter 7—A Little Change Is Not Enough

1. Benjamin and Rosamund Zander, *The Art of Possibility* (Boston: Harvard Business School Press, 2000), 125-26.

2. Anthony De Mello, *Taking Flight* (New York: Doubleday, 1988), 103.

3. John Gray, *Men Are from Mars, Women Are from Venus* (New York: Harper-Collins Publishers, 1991), 13.

4. Keith Thompson, "The Meaning of Being Male—A Conversation with Robert Bly," *L.A. Weekly* (August 5-11, 1983): 16.

5. Gray, *Men Are from Mars*, 133.

Chapter 8—Don't Be Afraid

1. Jerri Nielsen, *Ice Bound* (New York: Hyperion, 2001), 6.

2. Ibid., 193.

3. Watty Piper, *The Little Engine That Could* (New York: Platt & Munk). The book was first published in 1930.

4. Susan Jeffers, *Feel the Fear and Do It Anyway* (New York: Fawcett Columbine, 1987), 14-15.

5. Ibid., 22-28.

6. Gavin De Becker, *The Gift of Fear* (New York: Dell Publishing, 1997), 341.

7. Harriet Goldhor Lerner, *The Dance of Deception* (New York: HarperCollins, 1993), 187.

Chapter 9—Your Inner Voice

1. Harriet Goldhor Lerner, *The Dance of Deception* (New York: HarperCollins, 1993), 118.

2. Robert Wicks, *Touching the Holy* (Notre Dame, IN: Ave Maria Press, 1992), 68.

3. Ibid., 70.

4. Julia Cameron, *The Artist's Way* (New York: Putnam Publishing Group, 1992), 61.

5. Elizabeth O'Connor, *The Eighth Day of Creation: Gifts and Creativity* (Waco, TX: Word Books, 1971), 58.

6. Ibid.

7. Susan Jeffers, *Opening Our Hearts to Men* (New York: Fawcett Columbine, 1989), 158.

Chapter 10—The True Source of Power

1. Melody Beattie, *The Language of Letting Go* (San Francisco: Harper and Row Publishers, 1990), 123.

2. Benjamin and Rosamund Zanders, *The Art of Possibility* (Boston: Harvard Business School Press, 2000), 79.

3. Ibid., 89-90.

4. Henry Blackaby and Claude King, *Experiencing God* (Nashville: Broadman & Holman Publishers, 1994), 79.

5. Ibid., 83.

Chapter 11—Maintaining Your Momentum

1. Paulo Coelho, *The Alchemist* (San Francisco: HarperCollins Publishers, 1988), 11.

2. Stephen Lundin, Harry Paul, and John Christensen, *Fish* (New York: Hyperion, 1995).

3. Stephen Covey, *The Seven Habits of Highly Effective People* (New York: Simon & Schuster, 1989), 98.

4. Ibid.

5. Ibid., 107.

6. Robert Morris, "A Home for Love to Dwell: Covenant Relationship as Continual Conversion," *Weavings* 18, no. 2 (March/April 2003): 16.

7. Ibid., 20.

Also by David Hawkins

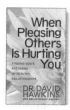

When Pleasing Others Is Hurting You

When you begin to forfeit your own God-given calling and identity in an unhealthy desire to please others, you move from servanthood to codependency. This helpful guide can get you back on track.

When the Man in Your Life Can't Commit

With empathy and insight Dr. Hawkins uncovers the telltale signs of commitment failure, why the problem exists, and how you can respond to and create a life with the commitment-phobic man you love.

Nine Critical Mistakes Most Couples Make

Dr. Hawkins shows that complex relational problems usually spring from nine destructive habits couples fall into, and he offers practical suggestions for changing the way husbands and wives relate to each other.

Saying It So He'll Listen

Dr. Hawkins offers straightforward, intelligent counsel for dealing with sensitive topics in a relationship. Readers will find new motivation to press through to the goal of effective communication: reconciliation and greater intimacy in marriage.

Does Your Man Have the Blues?

Dr. Hawkins exposes the problem of male depression with unusual compassion and clarity. He describes the telltale signs, pinpoints some of the causes, and offers suggestions to those who would help.

Dr. Hawkins is interested in hearing about your journey and may be contacted through his website at www.YourRealtionshipDoctor.com